5, 50

W9-CNC-079

The
Greyhound

An Owner's Guide To

A HAPPY HEALTHY PET

Howell Book House

Howell Book House
A Simon & Schuster Macmillan Company
1633 Broadway
New York, NY 10019

Copyright © 1998 by **Howell Book House**
All rights reserved. No part of this book may be reproduced or transmitted in any form or by any means, electronic or mechanical, including photocopying, recording, or by any information storage and retrieval system, without permission in writing from the Publisher.

MACMILLAN is a registered trademark of Macmillan, Inc.

Library of Congress Cataloging-in-Publication Data

Stern, Daniel Braun
  The greyhound: an owner's guide to a happy, healthy pet/ Daniel Braun Stern.
  p. cm
  ISBN: 0-087605-431-9 (hardcover)
  1. Greyhounds. I. Title. II. Series.
SF429.G8S74 1997
636.753'4—dc21

Manufactured in the United States of America
10 9 8 7 6 5 4 3 2 1

Series Director: Amanda Pisani
Assistant Series Director: Jennifer Liberts
Book Design: Michele Laseau
Cover Design: Iris Jeromnimon
Illustration: Laura Robbins and Jeff Yesh
Photography:
  Front cover and puppy by Steve Nash
  Back cover by Judith Strom
  Joan Balzarini: 26
  Paulette Braun/Pets by Paulette: 2–3, 11, 18, 27, 39
  Ringpress/Steve Nash: 6, 9, 13, 14, 15, 17, 32, 33, 47, 54, 63, 64, 65, 66, 67, 68, 73
  Judith Strom: 12, 19, 20, 22, 23, 25, 30–31, 43, 58, 60, 62, 72, 81
  Toni Tucker: 5, 7, 50
  Faith Uridel: 69
Production Team: John Carroll, Trudy Coler, Stephanie Hammett, Clint Lahnen, Dennis Sheehan and Terri Sheehan

Contents

part one

Welcome to the World of the Greyhound

1 What Is a Greyhound? 5

2 The Greyhound's Ancestry 13

3 The World According to the Greyhound 20

part two

Living with a Greyhound

4 Bringing Your Greyhound Home 32

5 Feeding Your Greyhound 54

6 Grooming Your Greyhound 62

7 Keeping Your Greyhound Healthy 68

part three

Enjoying Your Dog

8 Basic Training 98
by Ian Dunbar, Ph.D., MRCVS

9 Getting Active with Your Dog 128
by Bardi McLennan

10 Your Dog and Your Family 136
by Bardi McLennan

11 Your Dog and Your Community 144
by Bardi McLennan

part four

Beyond the Basics

12 Recommended Reading 151

13 Resources 155

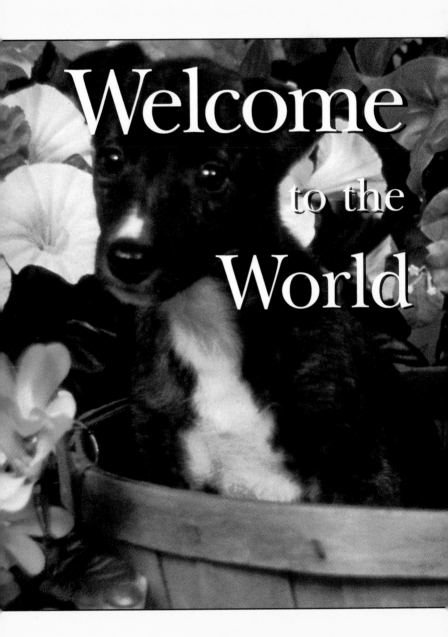

Welcome to the World

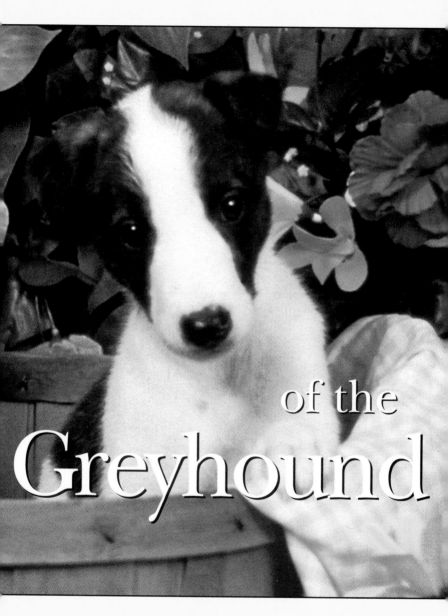

of the
Greyhound

External Features of the Greyhound

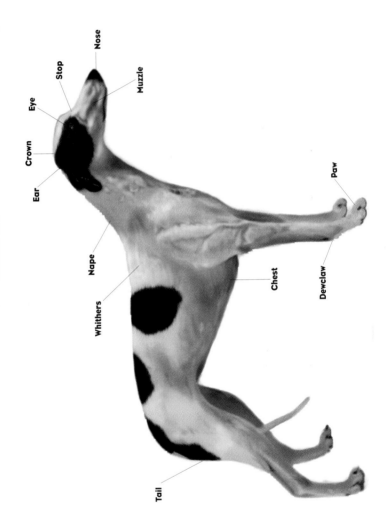

- Nose
- Muzzle
- Stop
- Eye
- Crown
- Ear
- Nape
- Whithers
- Chest
- Paw
- Dewclaw
- Tail

chapter 1

What Is a Greyhound?

The Greyhound is an ancient breed of dog that was originally bred to hunt animals ranging from rabbits to gazelles. He belongs to a family of dogs known as sighthounds; they hunt by sight rather than by scent. Some of the Greyhound's commonly known cousins include the Whippet, the Afghan Hound and the Irish Wolfhound. The Greyhound's keen eyesight, coupled with his long legs and deep chest, allow him to run with great speed in pursuit of his prey.

Greyhound Organizations

Two organizations are involved in the registration of purebred Greyhounds: the American Kennel Club (AKC), which registers Greyhounds for showing, and the National Greyhound Association (NGA), which registers Greyhounds for racing. While both AKC and NGA Greyhounds are purebred, they have been bred to do two very different things. The result is that although they share many physical characteristics in common, they have differences, too.

The Show Greyhound

Let's start off with an examination of the show Greyhound. Dog shows are a relatively new invention hav-

In a dog show, the Greyhound is judged on how close he comes to the breed standard.

ing started in the mid-1800s. The Greyhounds who existed for thousands of years before then were bred to hunt and later to course. Coursing is a sport that pits two Greyhounds against each other in pursuit of the game, usually a rabbit. Coursing is practiced on an open field, and dogs are judged not only on speed but on agility, determination and concentration.

When dog shows were first developed, the idea was to show off specimens that best exemplified the attributes of each breed. To win in the show ring, a Greyhound needed to show that he would be a worthy competitor on the field. He needed straight, muscular legs, a deep chest with great lung capacity and keen eyes capable of seeing small game on the horizon. The ideal Greyhound had to be streamlined.

As time passed, attention was given to other points of the dog such as the set of the ears, the size and the color. All of these points were drawn up into what is known as the breed standard. Dogs that come closest to the breed standard are the winners in the show ring.

In terms of popularity, the AKC registered 218 Greyhounds in 1996, ranking this breed as number 120 out of the 143 recognized breeds.

When Greyhounds are at attention their ears are semi-pricked.

The Standard

The standard describes the *ideal* Greyhound. Remember that no animal lives up to the standard in every way, although breeders keep striving to come as close to this description as possible. Greyhounds were among the earliest breeds shown at American dog shows. The first entry at Westminster Kennel Club show in 1877 included only eighteen Greyhounds.

Here is the AKC's breed standard for the Greyhound as written by the Greyhound Club of America. Comments that explain the standard in a little more detail follow.

HEAD

Long and narrow, fairly wide between the ears, scarcely perceptible stop, little or no development of nasal sinuses, good length of muzzle, which should be powerful without coarseness. Teeth very strong and even in front.

The overall effect should be one of refinement. Overshot or undershot jaws are to be avoided as are Roman noses or excessively wide or narrow skulls.

EARS

Small and fine in texture, thrown back and folded, except when excited, when they are semi-pricked.

In repose Greyhounds possess so-called rose ears. Ears that are set permanently in a semi-pricked or pricked state are a fault.

EYES

Dark, bright, intelligent, indicating spirit.

Greyhound eyes should have a far-reaching, keen quality that reflects their superior eyesight.

NECK

Long, muscular, without throatiness, slightly arched, and widening gradually into the shoulder.

The neck should indicate grace as well as strength with the curve being gentle. The neck should be neither too short nor too thick.

SHOULDERS

Placed as obliquely as possible, muscular without being loaded.

A Greyhound's shoulders should not have an excessively muscled appearance nor should they be flat or slab-sided.

FORELEGS

Perfectly straight, set well into the shoulder, neither turned in nor out, pasterns strong.

If a Greyhound's forelegs turn in or out, the entire balance of the body is thrown off.

CHEST

Deep, and as wide as consistent with speed, fairly well-sprung ribs.

Again, a slab-sided appearance is to be avoided as is a chest that is too narrow or too wide.

BACK

Muscular and broad, well-arched.

Well-arched without being roach-backed. There should be no evidence of a sloping topline or a sway-back.

The Greyhound's back is muscular and well-arched.

LOINS

Good depth of muscle, well-cut up in the flanks.

A meaty appearance is to be avoided. Long, lean and sinewy muscles are desired.

HIND QUARTERS

Long, very muscular and powerful, wide and well-let down, well-bent stifles. Hocks well bent and rather close to ground, wide but straight fore and aft.

It is essential that the hind quarters reflect the power and speed of the Greyhound but also give a refined impression. The rear legs should be neither bowed nor cow-hocked.

FEET

Hard and close, rather more hare than cat feet, well-knuckled up with good strong claws.

The feet need to be upright and not flat or splayed.

TAIL

Long, fine and tapering with a slight upward curve.

COAT

Short, smooth and firm in texture.

COLOR

Immaterial.

WEIGHT

Dogs, 65 to 70 pounds; bitches, 60 to 65 pounds.

Points

Greyhounds are judged in the ring on an overall picture with the Scale of Points being as follows:

General symmetry and quality	10
Head and neck	20
Chest and shoulders	20
Back	10
Quarters	20
Legs and feet	20
TOTAL	100

Remember that at dog shows, dogs are being judged not only against the others of their breed but against the breed standard. A complete description of the AKC standard for the Greyhound is available by writing to the American Kennel Club, 5580 Centerview Dr., Suite 200, Raleigh, NC 27606-3390.

Judging for Speed

Greyhounds registered with the National Greyhound Association are judged by an entirely different standard, namely, speed. As long as it is ascertained that a particular Greyhound is the product of two purebred registered Greyhounds, then he, too, is eligible for registration. But, instead of pursuing life in the show ring, he is destined for life on the racetrack.

An AKC Greyhound has less muscular definition because he isn't competitive on the track.

Size, color, sex or conformation are of no interest to the racing authorities. However, it stands to reason that dogs who are the best physical specimens will also be the ones who have the best chances of succeeding at the track. Keep in mind that approximately 39,000 Greyhounds are registered each year with the NGA, and many thousands of them display both tremendous speed and great beauty.

Since the form of a dog in the show ring is supposed to reflect its function in the world, then a case can be made for NGA Greyhounds conforming closest to the original purpose of the breed. A dog with an excessively narrow chest, for example, would have less lung capacity and, hence, not have the endurance to run as fast or as long. And certainly one with cow-hock–shaped hind legs might well trip over himself.

AKC and NGA Greyhounds

In the end, it becomes a matter of preference. NGA Greyhounds tend to be smaller and, after their training at the track, highly muscled and limber. AKC Greyhounds are often larger, have less defined muscles and are less competitive at field events. Attributes of both NGA and AKC Greyhounds are the combination of both nature and nurture. The qualities of either lineage can be emphasized or not, depending on the plan of the dog's owner.

The Greyhound's sweet temperament makes him a wonderful companion.

Temperament

Of course, no matter what type of Greyhound you choose, you are in for a treat. As a breed, the Greyhound is an affectionate, gentle, graceful creature that has kept human beings company for thousands of years. It is, perhaps, because of the Greyhound's long history of domesticity that they are among the most companionable dogs.

chapter 2

The Greyhound's Ancestry

Unlike most breeds of dog, the history of the Greyhound is so long and glorious that condensing it into one chapter can give you only a hint of all that it can lay claim to. Almost since the beginning of recorded history, there have been Greyhound-like dogs aiding human beings in the development of civilization.

They were Greyhound-like dogs because, although they had the characteristic long legs, deep chests and narrow heads, it is impossible to say with certainty which one of the many related strains of sighthounds they were. We do know that as early as 6000 B.C. dogs of this sort were depicted helping with the hunt in a drawing on the wall of a temple in what is now Turkey. Several thousand years later Greyhounds showed up on a funerary vase in the ancient kingdom of Susa.

13

The Ancient Greyhound

In Ancient Egypt, however, Greyhounds played roles not only as assistants for hunting but as household pets and highly revered beings. The Egyptian god Anubis was a deity who measured the deeds of a person's life at the moment of his or her death. In the carvings, called hieroglyphics, that the ancient Egyptians left behind, Anubis was represented as a Greyhound.

The Greyhound was revered by ancient Egypt-ians and consid-ered an honored part of the family.

Apparently the Egyptians translated their worship of Anubis into a very high regard for the real thing. Greyhounds lived in houses with their human families, they were mummified upon death and it is said that the death of a Greyhound was second in importance only to the death of a son. King Tutankhamen and Queen Cleopatra were among the many rulers of Egypt who kept Greyhounds, and the walls of some ancient tombs are decorated with drawings and praises of the owners' favorite Greyhounds.

PORTRAYAL IN LITERATURE

Many notable writers in ancient Greece discussed the finer points of Greyhounds. In *The Odyssey*, which was written around the year 800 B.C., Homer tells the story of Odysseus who, after having been away from his homeland for twenty years is recognized only by his faithful Greyhound, Argos. This, by the way, is the first time a dog was mentioned in literature.

Sport Coursing

The sport of coursing was popular in ancient Greece and Greyhounds were active participants. In A.D. 124 the Greek-born historian Arrian wrote, "The true sportsman does not take out his dogs to destroy the hares, but for the sake of the course and the contest between the dogs and the hares, and is glad if the hare escapes." Although his advice was not particularly well-received in its day, most coursing today is conducted using an artificial lure. Greyhounds, and indeed all sighthounds, are so keen on the chase that it doesn't really matter to them whether they are pursuing a live rabbit or a white plastic bag. And so plastic bags or animal hides are the lure of choice for the vast majority of coursing clubs in this country.

The keen eyesight of Greyhounds makes them excellent lure chasers.

Many Greek vases were decorated with scenes of Greyhounds in pursuit of a hare while others show the dogs accompanying their master to war. Greyhounds also figured in Greek mythology, especially in the tale of Actaeon and Artemis. As the story goes, Artemis was so enraged that Actaeon spied on her while she was bathing that she turned him into a stag then set her forty-eight Greyhounds on him!

15

The Evolving Greyhound

From Greece, the Greyhound made his way into the empire of ancient Rome. It was here that Greyhounds blossomed, for not only were they kept in homes but also they were given regular food. At earlier times in history they were afforded shelter but had to forage for food. Roman soldiers also took Greyhounds with them as they conquered new countries, and in this way the Greyhound spread throughout Europe, Great Britain and Ireland.

Ovid, the Roman poet who lived around the time of the birth of Christ, was familiar enough with Greyhounds to have included descriptions of them in his "Metamorphoses." He wrote:

> As when the impatient Greyhound, slipped
>   from far,
> Bounds o'er the glade to course the fearful hare
> She in her speed does all her safety lie,
> And he with double speed pursues his prey.

GREYHOUNDS IN ROME

Romans, too, included Greyhounds in their mythology. In a story closely resembling the Greek tale of Actaeon and Artemis, the Roman version involves Diana, the goddess of the hunt, and her friend, Procris. When Procris and his Greyhound, Lelaps, set off in the woods in pursuit of a hare, the gods watching the action decided to spare the hare's life. They accomplished this by turning it, and Lelaps, into stone.

By the time the Roman empire had begun to collapse, the Greyhound had been taken to every reach of its influence. The English, Irish and French took special delight in these dogs and many of their rulers kept

---

FAMOUS OWNERS OF GREYHOUNDS

King Tutankhamen

Alexander the Great

King Henry VIII

King Louis XV

Queen Victoria

General George Custer

Sir Walter Scott

Bo Derek

Greyhounds. In fact, for nearly 400 years, Greyhounds became the exclusive domain of the nobility. Peasants who somehow managed to obtain a Greyhound were punished severely. If it was discovered that they had stolen the dog, the punishment was death. If it was their own animal, the dog herself was punished by having several of her toes removed, a procedure called expedition. Apparently the idea behind that cruel measure was to see to it that the commoner's dog could not compete with the nobleman's Greyhounds for game on the nobleman's land.

Renaissance Dogs

As western civilization moved out of the dark ages into the Renaissance, artists began incorporating Greyhounds into their works. Examples can be found in paintings and sculptures by such notable artists as

Greyhounds are the first breed of dog mentioned in English literature.

Veronese, Pisanello and Uccello. In literature, Geoffrey Chaucer mentions the Greyhound in *The Canterbury Tales.* This is another first for the Greyhound: the first breed of dog mentioned in English literature. Later on, Shakespeare, too, writes of them in *King Lear, Henry IV* and *Henry V.*

The period of exploration that began with Christopher Columbus also saw the presence of Greyhounds. They accompanied him on his explorations to the New World where they were used mainly as canine bodyguards. Greyhounds also participated in onshore hunting expeditions while accompanying various Spanish explorers in the Dominican Republic, Florida and Mexico. On the other side of the world, Greyhounds

17

were on board with the crew that sailed with Captain Cook in the South Pacific.

THE GREYHOUND ARRIVES

The Greyhound's big period of immigration into the United States took place in the 1800s as many people from Ireland and Britain began settling the Midwest and the West. They brought with them not only their Greyhounds but also their love of the sport of coursing. The open spaces were ideal territory to try out new Greyhounds against the local game. Sometimes the sport was pursued to rid the fields of rabbits that might compete for newly planted crops. At other times, however, it was done just for fun.

Greyhound racing, using a mechanically driven lure, was developed in the United States.

Not all Midwesterners found live-lure coursing fun and many objected to the bloodletting when the Greyhounds captured a rabbit. In a direct response to their opposition, in 1906, Owen Patrick Smith invented the first practical mechanically driven lure. Although in 1876 the English tried an experimental mechanical rabbit, the idea never caught on and it was quickly abandoned. Smith refined the device and, most importantly, set about promoting this new sport. The idea was that people could still enjoy watching the Greyhounds run but without the bloodshed. This was the start of Greyhound racing.

On the Track

From its humble origins, Greyhound racing has grown into the sixth most popular spectator sport. As of this writing there are forty-nine tracks in sixteen states. But in recent years, the image of the sport has been tarnished by reports of abuse both to dogs actively racing and to those facing the end of their careers. While some animal rights activists seek to abolish Greyhound racing entirely, others work to improve living conditions at the track and to find homes for the retiring dogs.

Only a decade ago, the idea of adopting a former racing Greyhound was, if not unheard of, then at least exotic. Most people had never seen a live Greyhound up close and it was commonly thought that they somehow did not make good pets. All of that has changed today and roughly 16,000 of these ex-racers have settled quite nicely into second careers as pampered pets.

The Greyhound industry has begun to make changes not only in the way the dogs live but also in providing for their post-track years. One big change is that the number of Greyhounds registered with the NGA has declined dramatically, dropping from approximately 49,000 to 39,000 a year. Many race tracks now provide an on-site adoption center and most seasonal tracks now hold dogs that won't be moving on until homes can be found.

Organized adoptions are an effort to improve the lives of retired racing Greyhounds.

The problem is not yet solved, however. Thirteen thousand ex-racers were still euthanized last year. And disturbing, verified reports continue to surface about Greyhounds being procured illegally and then used for cruel laboratory experiments. But compared to a decade ago, it is a whole new world for these dogs, and that world is definitely improving.

chapter 3

The **World** According to the **Greyhound**

In order to completely understand your new Greyhound, it is important to know where he came from. That means two things: knowing what his breed was developed for and what his immediate background is. If he is an AKC Greyhound, his immediate background is only an issue to the extent that you have checked the reputation of the breeder, have met your puppy's mother (dam) and possibly his father (sire) and have a certificate from a veterinarian certifying your puppy is in good health. Other than that,

Greyhound puppies receive the same level of care as any other breed.

The Former Racer

If your new Greyhound is a former racer, however, his immediate history is quite unlike that of any other breed. This chapter will explain how that history can affect him as a pet.

ANCESTRY

Let's start off with a look at why Greyhounds as a breed were developed. As was mentioned in chapter 1, Greyhounds are sighthounds; they hunt by sight rather than by scent. Until you've really seen this trait in action, though, it is hard to appreciate what this translates into in terms of your pet.

Everything about the physique of the Greyhound is designed for speed. If you take a look at your Greyhound right now you'll see what I mean. Apart from the obvious long legs and deep chest, there are also subtle signs. The narrow, wedge-shaped head, the thrown back ears, the long muscular toes and the strong whip-like tail are all examples of an aerodynamic design. At a time when people's very survival depended on their dog's ability to run down and capture game, the Greyhound, as one of the earliest breeds of dog, was well-suited to the task.

Because these early Greyhounds lived in lands consisting in large part of wide open plains, it was essential that they had the ability to see their prey easily. Whereas other dogs relied on the scent of their prey clinging to grass or shrubs, there was little chance of that happening in a sand-shifting desert. So, although anatomically the eyes of a Greyhound are no different from any other dog's, they have developed a reliance on their sight which lasts to this day.

CHARACTERISTICS OF THE GREYHOUND

strong running instinct

excellent eyesight

intolerant of temperature extremes

sensitive to criticism

gentle

affectionate

21

BUILT FOR SPEED

Although I have mentioned the speed at which a Greyhound is capable of running, I have not yet mentioned the top speed at which a Greyhound has been clocked: 42 miles per hour! In other words, they are only just slightly slower than a racehorse. Human beings, on the other hand, have a top speed of about 26 m.p.h. What this means is that if you are trying to catch a running Greyhound, forget it. First of all, if you run after him he may think you are chasing him and run even faster. Second of all, you'll never catch up.

Speed is one quality where ex-racing Greyhounds and the AKC version differ slightly. While the AKC Greyhounds are physically capable of the same speeds as their racing counterparts, they are subject only to their running instinct. Ex-racers, on the other hand, not only have the running instinct but, on top of that, the instinct has been reinforced by intensive training from the moment they were born.

With patient training, Greyhounds easily learn obedience commands.

I am not suggesting here that AKC Greyhounds are not as fast nor am I saying that they should ever be allowed to run loose except in a fenced area. What I am saying is that you have a somewhat better chance of teaching them the obedience commands of "Come" or "Stay"

and having the phrases mean something outside the classroom than you have with an ex-racer. Although ex-racers can learn these commands and they may even complete advanced obedience classes, if you are walking with your ex-racer off-lead and a chipmunk suddenly crosses his path, do not expect your commands to be heard. Thousands of years of instinct combined with an early puppyhood education of reinforcement add up to a running machine. Please do not harbor the mistaken impression that this can ever be completely erased.

Keep your Greyhound warm with a special coat when the temperature starts to drop.

SENSITIVE TO TEMPERATURE

One other thing about Greyhound ancestry that has a direct bearing on their lives as pets is their sensitivity to heat and cold. Greyhounds were developed in a warm climate and were taken inside at night. Greyhounds are dogs that have little body fat and a very fine coat. As such, there is nothing to insulate them from either the heat of summer or the cold of winter.

Greyhounds are house dogs exclusively. The ideal temperatures for them range from 65 to 75 degrees Fahrenheit. Do not leave them in a car during warm weather with the windows cracked because in a very short amount of time he will become too hot and could sicken or die. Likewise, even an insulated dog house will not be warm enough for greyhounds during cold weather. In fact, Greyhounds need protection from the cold even while out on their walks with you. The rule of thumb is that if it is cool enough for you to need a jacket or coat, it is cool enough for your greyhound to have one, too.

THE INSTINCT TO HUNT

One final note about Greyhounds' instinct and education that bears discussion here is the hunting instinct. Again, this is something that may be more pronounced in ex-racers than in AKC Greyhounds. All Greyhounds have a strong drive to run. What you need to keep in mind is that although they simply love to run, they also have a purpose in mind, namely, to catch whatever it is they are running after.

Historically, Greyhounds' prey have been rabbits, gazelles or even deer. Your Greyhound, however, will more likely be aiming for squirrels or rabbits in your backyard. In the worst case scenario, he could be aiming for your cat or small dog. Greyhounds are not necessarily more likely than any other breed to be unfriendly toward small pets but when they do decide to chase, they have a better than average chance of a successful catch.

GREYHOUNDS AND OTHER PETS

My experience with ex-racers has shown me that most are good with cats or small dogs. Some have no interest in chasing whatsoever and it is easy to see why they were relieved of their duties at the track. Others have an interest but it is just to play.

If your Greyhound's tail is wagging and he does not charge forward with blinding speed, he's not interested. The ones who are trouble are those who stare fixedly at their "prey" and, of course, those who practically pull your arm out of the socket trying to get at the desired creature. Either of these two types will be trouble for your small pets and there is little or no chance of training them out of it. Considering that the life of another animal is at stake, err on the side of caution and make sure the Greyhound you choose to bring into your home is small-animal friendly.

If you are buying a Greyhound puppy and are bringing him into a home with small animals, you should have no difficulty getting him to realize that the other animals are part of his pack and are to be respected. If you are adopting an older Greyhound, either an ex-show dog or an ex-racer, then it is wise to ascertain the dog's compatibility with small animals in advance.

The dog should either be tested or have actually lived with small animals, perhaps either in its previous home or in a foster home. One other thing to remember is that although a Greyhound may be perfectly good with small animals inside the house, outside may be another matter. For some dogs, the sight of a small dog or cat in the open air flips on the chase switch and it is just too much of a temptation to resist. Again, exercise caution.

COMPATIBILITY

As a breed, Greyhounds are neither dominant nor demanding. Perhaps more than other breeds, they seem to thrive on the company of other dogs, especially other Greyhounds. Anyone who has ever attended a reunion of retired racers is struck by the compatibility of dogs who have never even met each

other before. They seem to greet fellow ex-racers as long lost friends and, as they say, seldom is heard a discouraging word. Show Greyhounds also benefit from their ease with other dogs. For Greyhounds, the hustle and bustle of dog shows are not obstacles, and this can easily translate into a dog who is composed and focused in the show ring.

Greyhounds love to play and enjoy the companionship of other pets.

25

PEOPLE-LOVING DOGS

Most Greyhounds love the company of people as much as they love the company of other dogs. If a Greyhound is being kept as an only dog, it is especially important that he be given an extra amount of attention. The most difficult homes in which to place Greyhounds are the ones where there are no other pets and the owners work long hours. It is difficult for these dogs not to feel insecure or even abandoned under such circumstances. A possible antidote is a lunchtime visit. An even better solution is another dog so the two can keep each other company.

GREYHOUNDS ARE DOCILE

If it is true that your strength is also your weakness, then the lack of aggression displayed by most Grey-

Some Greyhounds have earned a reputation of being "couch potatoes."

hounds means that although they make docile, calm pets they are a very poor choice as watchdogs, guard dogs or, heaven forbid, attack dogs. Barking is rare in this breed but it is something they can learn from other dogs. A friend told me that he stopped by while I was not at home. My Greyhound was sleeping on the couch in full view of the front door yet, far from barking or growling, he never even lifted his head while "the intruder" knocked. My friend remarked that if he hadn't known better he would have thought that I had an 80-pound stuffed dog!

And, speaking of couches, it may seem odd that dogs who are capable of tremendous bursts of speed are such couch potatoes at home. Yet most people fail to realize that Greyhounds are sprinters, not long distance runners. Greyhound races, for example, are

⁵⁄₁₆ and ⁷⁄₁₆ of a mile. At the end of the race, the dogs are completely exhausted and incapable of running further. Slower breeds of dogs, which include the vast majority, may be able to last longer but they are incapable of the speed. As jogging companions, Greyhounds can gradually work up to a mile or two but they are poor candidates for longer distances.

GREYHOUNDS NEED CUSHIONING

Therefore, what Greyhounds may consider their reward for their great speed is an extremely soft life when they are not in motion. They love soft cushions, sofas and, best of all, your own bed for sleeping. They can, of course, be trained to sleep only in approved areas, but it is essential that a soft surface be available. Again, their lack of fur or natural padding makes them susceptible to pressure sores.

YOUR AFFECTIONATE GREYHOUND

Although Greyhounds are affectionate pets, they do not give big, sloppy kisses. They are also unlikely to give a howl of joy when you return home. The Greyhound style of affection is a wildly wagging tail when you return, and even wilder wags, perhaps accompanied by half-leaps, when you suggest going for a walk. They are quite eager to curl up next to you on a couch and rest their head in your lap. Many like to follow you from room to room, especially when newly adopted. Almost all can be counted on to be gentle, quiet, sweet-natured companions.

*The warm-hearted,
Greyhound style
of affection.*

27

More Information on Greyhounds

NATIONAL BREED CLUB

Greyhound Club of America (for AKC/show Greyhounds)
Ms. Marsha Wartell, Secretary
3433 Cartagena
Corpus Christi, TX 78418

REGISTRY OF ASSOCIATIONS

American Kennel Club (for show Greyhounds)
Registration and Information
5580 Centerview Drive, Ste. 200
Raleigh, NC 27606-3390
(919) 233-9767

National Greyhound Association (for racing Greyhounds)
P.O. Box 543
Abilene, KS 67410
(913) 263-4660

ADOPTION INFORMATION

Greyhound Pets of America (retired racers)
1-800-366-1472 (calls are forwarded to the chapter nearest to you)

Cheryl Reynolds, Rescue Chairman
Greyhound Club of America (AKC)
(805)684-4914

MAGAZINES

Celebrating Greyhounds: The Magazine
(general interest)
The Greyhound Project, Inc.
P.O. Box 173
Holbrook, MA 02343

Greyhound Review
(official publication of the NGA; see NGA address
above)

The Sighthound Review
(extensive show coverage)
P.O. Box 30430
Santa Barbara, CA 93130

BOOKS

Barnes, Julia, Editor. *The Complete Book of Greyhounds.*
New York: Howell Book House, 1994.

Blythe, Linda; James Gannon and Craig Morrie.
*Care of the Racing Greyhound: A Guide for Trainers,
Breeders and Veterinarians.* American Greyhound
Council (available through the NGA, address above).

Branigan, Cynthia A. *Adopting The Racing Greyhound.*
New York: Howell Book House, 1992.

Branigan, Cynthia A. *The Reign of the Greyhound: A
Popular History of the Oldest Family of Dogs.* New York:
Howell Book House, 1997.

VIDEOS

The Greyhound (#VVT411)
American Kennel Club (address above)

Soundness Examination of the Racing Greyhound
James Gannon
National Greyhound Association (address above)

SUPPLIES

Animal Magnetism
(Books, hard to find sighthound supplies, gifts)
P.O. Box 101
Lambertville, NJ 08530
1-800-836-2546

Living
with a

part two

Greyhound

chapter 4

Bringing Your Greyhound Home

Whether you are bringing home a Greyhound puppy or a retired racer, there are some basic guidelines to follow that will ease the transition of any dog into your life. Rule number one: Look before you leap.

Choosing to add a dog to your life is a big step, one that requires much thought. Thanks to better nutrition and veterinary advances, dogs are living longer lives than ever. Greyhounds, for example, can be expected to live twelve to fourteen years. As such, you need to take a long hard look at whether or not you are willing to make such a lengthy commitment.

Choosing the Right Dog for You

Assuming you are willing, the next decision is what kind of dog you want. I hope that this book will go a long way toward helping you get a feel for Greyhounds. They are not for everyone, no breed is. But if you decide Greyhounds are for you, then it's time to get your house in order.

Adopting a Puppy

The first thing to remember is to *have patience!* Your Greyhound is worth waiting for. Greyhound puppies are rarely found in pet shops. Since the supply of puppies is limited, a reputable breeder has no need to use a third party to market his or her pups.

What is a reputable breeder? First and foremost, he or she must have integrity and care about the dogs. How are the dogs housed? Are they clean? How do they react to their owner? Judging by the number of dogs, is this obviously a commercial project? Some commercial projects are acceptable, but it is the exception rather than the rule.

Puppies are adorable, but require extra care, training and socialization.

The "one-dog" backyard setup can be problematic, too. It really depends upon the operator in charge and his or her motivation. Are money and profits the priority or is there truly an interest in the welfare of the dogs? To be a successful, happy breeder, you must truly enjoy breeding and raising puppies, because it is *hard work!*

A breeder who really cares about his dogs will screen the potential buyer just as carefully as he, the breeder, is being screened. As a buyer, be truthful.

A pet-quality pup will probably cost less money than a potential show dog—but will not win in the show ring or produce quality pups. He will have just as much love and companionship to give as his blue-ribbon brothers.

It is important that everyone in the household agrees on adopting and devoting energy to raising a Greyhound puppy; sooner or later, each person will have to care for the dog.

Of course, you want to be sure your pup is registered with AKC or at least the registration has been applied for. You shouldn't hear, "He is purebred but we just never registered his mother," or, "His father is eligible but has not been registered." The owner (if reputable) of the male would not breed an unregistered female and vice versa. If you are unfortunate enough to find yourself in this situation, even though the puppies are inexpensive and are so cute (all puppies are cute), seem healthy and happy—STOP! Let your head control your heart and march your feet away quickly. Registration, like a trademark, gives some assurance of the final product. Only the very experienced breeder can detect cross breeding in tiny puppies. The breeder should give you at least a three-generation pedigree, as well as a health and shot record.

Don't Forget a Health Check

You should be allowed to take the pup or adult dog to a veterinarian of your choice within seventy-two hours for a health and physical exam. If the veterinarian finds anything wrong, i.e., heart murmur, cryptorchid, etc., the seller or breeder should take the dog back.

Again, it is very important to remember that a puppy is an eight- to twelve-year commitment, so your entire family should want her. Because your new Greyhound will become a family member, she must be loved and accepted for all of her good traits as well as her imperfections.

Most Greyhound breeders are sincere, honest people. They care about the welfare of their dogs and want only the best for you and the dog. Take time and find the puppy that is just what you have been dreaming about and enjoy the love and devotion that is complete and without judgment.

FINDING A BREEDER

How do you find a breeder if you do not have personal knowledge of one or know someone who has a Greyhound? Ask the local veterinarian, boarding kennels, pet supply stores or owners and breeders of other breeds. Answer ads in papers, but carefully check out the advertiser before you purchase your puppy this way: Write to the American Kennel Club and ask for their list of breeders and for the address of the Greyhound Dog Club of America, which will direct you to breeders in your part of the country.

Surely, one or more of these will be able to give you leads to more than one breeder. Early spring is probably the best time to look for a puppy, and early summer is the best time to get a puppy. The supply of puppies is usually greater in the spring of the year. Most animals' breeding cycle, like the renewal of plant life, begins in the spring. Also, it is much easier to housetrain a puppy in warm weather. Neither you nor the puppy want to trek out of doors in cold weather so the puppy can take care of her bodily functions (especially in the middle of the night).

You have decided you do want a Greyhound. You have read the standard and you have found a nice litter of puppies bred by a reputable breeder. These puppies are or will be AKC registered. You have seen their mother and have been given the history of their father.

IS A PUPPY OKAY FOR MY FAMILY?

Greyhounds are good with children but eight-week-old puppies and babies under two years are not a good combination. The puppy and the child are both too immature to understand the limitations of the other. If there are children under two years of age, I suggest you look for a puppy at least six months old or a young adult dog. It is not true that a pup must grow up with a child to accept the child. With a little time and a little patience, even an older dog can be taught.

WHAT COLOR?

You had your heart set on a white puppy but there are no white puppies. Should you look further for the white puppy? If the only thing that is preventing you from selecting one of these puppies is color, then I suggest you select the next best puppy. By that I mean the one that pleases you most in this particular litter and that the breeder will sell. Color really is not important, and soon you will have forgotten you ever wanted a white puppy when the one you have finds her way into your heart.

MALE OR FEMALE?

Should you get a male or a female? Because you will be sure to neuter your pet Greyhound, males and females make equally good pets. Neutering prevents many problems as your Greyhound grows older.

SO WHAT IS IMPORTANT?

In a few words, select an outgoing, vigorous, playful puppy regardless of color or sex.

If you were planning to use your puppy for breeding, then the number and quality of champions in her pedigree would be a selling point. But your pup is going to be a companion, so champion parents and the number of champions in her family tree are not important. It is important that she is AKC-registered, healthy and a good specimen of the breed.

WHEN TO BRING YOUR PUPPY HOME

Select a time when you will be at home for several days. Your puppy needs to get to know you, to become acclimated to her new home and crate, to get comfortable with her daily schedule of walks, play time and perhaps new food (don't change food unless absolutely necessary for several days and then change gradually).

She needs some free time just to explore. She needs to be held and loved. Just imagine yourself in her place. Your puppy can't talk and she can't really understand what you are saying. Everything is new and different. It takes time, and the time that is spent now will help her to be a happy, confident animal living a wonderful life of giving, because she trusts you and knows she is wanted.

Holidays

It is not wise to get a new puppy at holiday time. First, the house is certainly not on any kind of a schedule. Christmas trees are fascinating but certainly a no-no. Wrapping paper, packages, pins and ribbons are all likely to be on the floor; these can not only be dangerous for your puppy, but she may also upset some family members with her explorations into their packages. Don't tempt her. A puppy is a baby, and she will get tired of being handled and played with by many different people. If you must get or take her at holiday time, then be sure she has a crate in a nice, quiet, warm place. Do not allow everyone to hold her and don't be guilty of showing her to everyone who comes to visit. Remember, she is a confused, bewildered baby.

If you have gotten an adult dog, the same plan should be followed. She may be a grown-up dog, but she doesn't understand why she has a new home or where her former owner is. She needs time to bond with you and feel safe and wanted.

WHAT KIND OF HOME DOES YOUR PUPPY NEED?

A fenced-in area where the puppy will be safe, and which the neighbors accept, is almost a must. Just as you need a little private time in your bathroom to contemplate the problems of the world, so does the puppy need a little private time to run about off-lead and smell all the wonderful, interesting scents about her. She needs to sit in the sun, watch the birds, get a fresh drink of water and maybe take a little snooze. A concrete run will do, but a little green grass to stretch out on is heaven. This does not eliminate the need to go for a walk but it certainly makes housetraining and caring for toilet needs simpler. A pooper-scooper is also necessary to help keep the area clean. A clean area will not attract flies or nasty remarks from the neighbors. Check carefully for any poisonous weeds, shrubs or plants.

DO NOT SPRAY the dog run with insecticides or herbicides. Some of these chemicals may damage the dog's immune system. Many people have to fertilize and spray their lawn for weeds; it is very important to keep dogs and people off the grass for at least seventy-two hours after treatment to avoid any problems.

Necessary Equipment

There are certain supplies needed to help you and the puppy prepare for a satisfying and long life together.

Baby Gates

You should decide before you bring your puppy home just how much freedom she will have in the house. Will she be free to go any place or will boundaries be established?

If certain parts of your home are to be off-limits, there are good, attractive baby gates on the market. Some are built so there is a gate within the gate and all you have to do is open this gate when you need to go through it. This type is probably the most practical. It is very difficult for a dog to observe a nonexistent barrier that keeps her from someplace she wants to go.

Crate Training

With a small puppy, it is best to confine her to specific areas until she is completely "house-trained". She could come into the family room for a short time and under constant supervision right after she has done her "duty" outside. The ideal plan is to have a place where she can be confined in the kitchen or utility area, someplace where she is a part of the family. As she grows and matures, she will be allowed more freedom.

The easiest and most effective way is to get an appropriately sized crate with padding for the Greyhound's special structure. Place it where the puppy is to sleep, and make sure this place is warm and free of drafts. Confine the puppy except for definite play and exercise time for the first few days. Leave the door open when the puppy is out so she can return at will. There crate should have pans that clip on its sides for food and water. The pup should always have fresh water available.

Food and Water Dishes

Bowls of stainless steel or other metal are ideal. But heavy plastic or "crock" type work as well. Some dogs enjoy picking up their pan and tossing it about after they have finished eating. Scattered food is nothing more than a mess—but spilled water cannot satisfy thirst.

It won't take long until your puppy has picked out her favorite toys.

Toys

Soft toys and "chew" bones make life a little more interesting when the dog is alone. Hard-rubber bones and real sterilized bones can be purchased from a pet shop and are safe and acceptable. Some soft toys are safe. Check the squeaker; if it is metal, it must be taken out or the toy left in the store. (The metal squeaker can be a choking hazard.)

You can make soft toys for your Greyhound. A child's tube sock stuffed full of strips of nylon panty hose or any strips of well worn rags and then sewn shut is an ideal toy. Dogs may grab this, throw it up, try to catch it, tease, etc. When it is dirty, toss it into the washer. Washed, rinsed and dried, it becomes new again, or if it is worn out, toss it away. Little money has been involved. Be sure any balls are too large for the dog to swallow and not made of foam rubber that can be broken into chunks. Safety is the watchword.

Do not give an old shoe to become a toy. Then any shoe—new, never worn or old and unwearable—is the same to the dog and sooner or later your brand-new shoe becomes a toy.

CHOOSING A VETERINARIAN

Finally, before you bring your puppy home, select a veterinarian to care for her health. Select the veterinarian as you would your own private physician or pediatrician. Not only his or her veterinary knowledge but availability should be considered, too. Since your Greyhound is not going to be shown or used for breeding, spaying the female should be considered. This prevents the twice-a-year need of confining and watching her very closely during her heat periods. Also, statistics prove that breast cancer and pyometra (uterine infection) are less likely to occur in spayed females. Neutered males are less aggressive and less likely to "mark" the furniture.

Discuss this care of your dog with your veterinarian, he is better able to advise you than the next-door neighbor or the man down the street.

Adopting an Ex-Racer

If you are bringing home an ex-racer, the dog's formative years were spent in intensive training, first at a breeding farm and later at a training kennel. You can't undo what has been done but, remember, not all that was done was bad. In fact, a great deal of it was quite good and has made life a lot easier for you.

Life at the track is not life at home, but these Greyhounds were not pets, they were professional athletes. A certain amount of discipline is necessary in order to keep the dogs focused and in racing condition. The same is true, of course, of professional show dogs. Those Greyhounds who travel the show circuit across the country do not have the same kind of life as a household pet. It is inaccurate to characterize it as bad; it's just different.

For a complete discussion of what life is like at the track for Greyhounds and what it is like to bring one home, I highly recommend the book *Adopting the Racing Greyhound* by Cynthia A. Branigan (New York: Howell Book House, 1992). I cannot imagine adopting a Greyhound without having this book as a guide. Most adoption agencies consider it required reading as it makes their job easier and benefits the dogs and their new families greatly.

The following are some of the ways in which your ex-racer's early training can help you today:

- Greyhounds at the track sleep in large crates. Bedding usually consists of either carpet remnants or shredded newspaper. Most trainers let the dogs out to relieve themselves four times a day. What this means for you is that although an ex-racer is not housebroken they are cratetrained. Provided you follow at least a four-times-a-day turnout schedule, you should have little difficulty housebreaking your dog in no time.

- Another bit of education they received at the track that comes in handy for you is their leash training. Most Greyhound puppies get their first collar at 4 months and are leash trained beginning at 8 months of age. The advantage to you is obvious. Anyone expecting an ex-racer to be more like a bucking bronco is in for a pleasant surprise. Most are extremely tractable on lead. For the very small minority who are not, the use of a training halter that fits around the neck then under the arms provides an easy, humane method of getting them to stop pulling. After a few sessions the halter is usually no longer needed.

- One of the other ways in which your ex-racer's early life now serves him, and you, is the fact that she is used to being handled. Life at the track is a whirlwind of activity. The dogs are groomed, weighed, fitted with muzzles, examined by veterinarians, walked, loaded into kennel trucks and generally very much a part of all that is going on.

- Similarly, track Greyhounds are used to being around other dogs. This is especially useful if you are considering introducing an ex-racer into a home that already has dogs. Not only are track Greyhounds comfortable with other dogs, but most really enjoy the company.

HELPING YOUR GREYHOUND ADJUST

Of course for all of the ways in which their early lives have prepared them for life in the home, there is probably an equal number of ways that they are totally unprepared for life in the real world.

Windows? Never saw them. Stairs? Don't know what they are. Children? What are children? These are but a few of the everyday things that ex-racers must be introduced to. These difficulties are not insurmountable, but with patience and understanding, they can easily be overcome.

Windows

Taking these new things one at a time, let's start with windows. How, you might ask, can they never have seen a window? The answer is that Greyhounds at the track are either inside their crate or outside with others of their own sex in a turnout pen. There are no windows in either place. When they ride from track to track in kennel trucks they are in individual compartments that feature louvered doors. No windows there either. The only other place they are is on the track and, needless to say, there is no need for windows there.

The easiest way to introduce ex-racers to windows is to walk them up to one, tap on it or press their paw gently against it. That way you'll be sure they really know it's there. There have been cases of ex-racers running into glass not realizing it was solid. Such a mishap can result in the dog being knocked out or cut. It's much easier just to make formal introductions when your dog first comes into your home.

Stairs

Stairs are foreign to ex-racers because everything is flat at the track. But don't feel this is a difficult challenge. Most Greyhounds learn in a few days how to go up and down with ease. This is accomplished even more quickly if you can get them to feel that they are missing out on all of the fun (i.e., food, the human's bed, etc.) by not negotiating the steps.

To teach them how to use stairs is very easy. To get them to go up, get behind them and gently push on their rump. Most will somehow step up first one, then two and, finally, all the stairs. To get them to go down, get in front of them and, while tugging on their collar, coax them down. Many find it easier to go up than down, but eventually they all get the hang of it.

Teaching children to respect your Greyhound's limits is the first step of a harmonious relationship.

Children

As for children, while most Greyhounds have not seen them before, the majority of dogs accept them readily. The gentle nature of these dogs is such that they are unlikely to snap at a child. When they do, it is often the result of the parents' inattention to the child's behavior or the warning signs from the dog.

Whole books have been written on the subject of children and dogs. The one I like best is *Childproofing Your Dog* by Brian Kilcommons (New York: Warner Books, 1995). The basic premise is really to train the parents, but Kilcommons discusses at length how to read the warning signs that a dog gives

43

when she feels threatened, afraid or has just had enough. Everyone with children and dogs should read this book.

Greyhounds are a gentle breed, but any dog has her limits. Children need to be taught to respect a dog's privacy. In the case of ex-racers, children also need to be taught that when the dog is asleep you must never touch them, or worse yet, hug them, without first waking them up by calling their name.

The reason for this is that at the track, Greyhounds sleep in crates. Never in their lives are they touched while they are asleep. To do so now might easily frighten the dog and, while still half asleep, they could respond with a snap. This is not a malicious act, really. It is simply instinct. Knowing this fact about their history allows you to make the necessary changes in your behavior.

Crates

A crate is the one essential tool that every Greyhound owner should have. There are two ways that crates are useful: They provide a sanctuary for the dog and they aid in the housebreaking process.

Let's look at the sanctuary part first. As pointed out earlier, puppies need time out. Crates are the ideal place for them to get just that. It is a space where a puppy can relax, sleep or just watch the activities of the human family without having to participate. You are also training your puppy to be a better mannered pet. At some point, the veterinarian, groomer or housesitter may really appreciate that your dog is cratetrained.

Ex-racers have spent all of their lives in crates. Many people who adopt consider it their duty to free them of what they consider the equivalent of dog prison. These people, however, do not understand that a crate is not a punishment but really more like the dog's own apartment or bedroom.

Most ex-racers accept their crates willingly. The ones who don't are simply trying to see what they can get over on their new owners. A firm "Kennel up" command accompanied, if necessary, by a push on the rump is usually all they need. Remember, when you tell your dog to do something you have to mean it. Dogs are very clever about knowing when you are waffling!

For ex-racers, the crate is the place to be when you are not at home. They can get into a lot of trouble if you give them the run of the house before they are house-broken and acclimated to their new surroundings. Crates are for the dog's safety and for your peace of mind while you are not around to supervise your dog's activities.

By the way, if you think locking your ex-racer in a laundry room or putting a gate across the kitchen is a reasonable substitute for a crate, guess again. Most ex-racers are far more comfortable in a crate than in either of the other two choices. Some panic and begin the gnaw the woodwork or claw at the door. Others will jump a gate and tear up the rest of your house. In an informal survey I conducted, the people across the country who adopted ex-racers and then returned them were, almost without exception, people who would not use a crate.

TYPES OF CRATES

There are two kinds of crates: wire and molded plastic. The wire variety is usually collapsible, costs quite a bit more than the plastic type and, if a dog really puts her mind to it, is capable of being bent to allow escape. The molded plastic type is what is used by airlines and you can bet they are not interested in dogs who are able to escape. It also provides more of a den-like atmosphere, which is what dogs, by nature, are most comfortable with.

Most Greyhounds will fit into a 500 size crate (extra large), while a small percentage of the larger males may need a 700 size (giant). (Inexplicably, no one makes a 600 size!)

Using a Crate for Housebreaking

The use of a crate for housebreaking is self-explanatory. Unless you are able to keep an eye on a dog who isn't housebroken, she should be in a crate. When she is not, you need to look for warning signs that she needs to go out. These include pacing, whimpering, walking in circles or going to the door. Dogs should always be let out first thing in the morning, last thing at night and after each meal. If you are in the house and the dog disappears from sight, find her. She may be in a back bedroom looking for a private spot to relieve herself. If you find her lurking somewhere, take her out and, most importantly, give her lots of praise when she is successful.

The final word on crates: Crates are not a punishment. They are to aid you in housebreaking and are the dog's private condo. A crate is not a dungeon nor is it a place to keep a dog confined for more than eight hours at a time. My own preference is to get your dog gradually used to being uncrated after she is used to your schedule and is completely housebroken. If you can arrange to test your dog for short periods, say, five or ten minutes uncrated, and then gradually lengthen it, you will know if she is ready for the run of the house.

Preparing for Your Greyhound's Arrival

There are some supplies you will need to have on hand before you bring home your Greyhound. This brings me to rule number two: Be prepared. Don't go out on a shopping expedition after the dog is in your home. Get your supplies in advance so you can spend all of your time with your new companion.

A crate should be at the top of your list, of course. If you have time, try ordering it from a wholesale mail order company because this can save you a lot of money. If not, try one of the large chains of pet supply stores because their prices are second best. Check-out all available sizes to find the best fit for your Greyhound.

Food and Water Dishes

Next you will need two dishes, one for food and one for water. Water, of course, should be available at all times.

Two Comfortable Beds

Two soft beds, preferably with washable covers, should be next on your list. One should be placed in the room you spend the most time in so that the dog can be with you and be comfortable. The other should be placed in the dog's crate. Remember, soft bedding is not a luxury for Greyhounds, it is a necessity.

Soft beds are essential for keeping your Greyhound comfortable.

Collar and Leash

Most adoption groups, or breeders, will supply a collar and matching leash for your dog. If not you will need to get your own. There is only one type of collar for a Greyhound: a humane safety collar. The width of a Greyhound's head is roughly the same as her neck. For that reason, if you use a standard buckle-type collar you run the risk of losing your dog if she backs out of her collar. If you ever have the misfortune of seeing a Greyhound get frightened and back out of her collar and take off, you'll know what I mean.

Humane safety collars are similar to choke collars except that they tighten on two points and thus restrain without pinching or choking. These collars are generally not available in pet supply stores but are carried by sighthound specialty mail order companies.

IDENTIFICATION TAGS

Another necessary item to get in advance is an identification tag. It is not necessary to have your dog's name on the collar. What is necessary is your name, address and phone number, including area code. Again, most adoption groups provide a tag with their name and number, but you need one of your own, too.

COATS

As was discussed in an earlier chapter, coats, too, are a necessity for Greyhounds if they are to be exposed to temperatures cool enough for you to need one. This is hard to buy in advance since you want to get the right fit. My advice is to bring an old sweatshirt with you if you are picking up your dog on a chilly day. It will do for short periods until you get an accurate measurement.

When buying a coat, try to get one designed for Greyhounds. A Golden Retriever, for example, may wear a coat of the same length, but it will be ungainly on a Greyhound. Again, a sighthound specialty business is your best bet for coats.

RETRIEVAL DEVICES

Squawkers are devices that, when blown into, imitate the sound of a rabbit in distress. They are handy to have in the event that you ever need to retrieve your Greyhound. They are not a sure thing, of course, but they do get the dog's attention if she is within earshot, and it might just be long enough for you to grab her.

PUPPYPROOFING

If you have adopted a puppy, or a very inquisitive ex-racer, you must make sure your house, yard and garage are safe for your new Greyhound. You'd be surprised what a curious puppy or bored adult dog can get into. In the house, crawl around on your hands and knees and look at things from a dog's viewpoint. Do you see knickknacks within reach? Are there books or magazines to chew on? Are there dangling electrical cords that could be tempting to gnaw on? Puppies especially are fascinated by extension and lamp cords. Chewing these could result in electrocution of the dog or starting a fire. If the pup is to be left alone where lamp cords or extension cords are, then the cords must be disconnected and put away. However, if you are going to be with her, leave the cords in their regular places. She must be taught to leave the cords alone. This requires time and persistence. Give her a stern "NO" every time she goes near the cords. After all, you share this house, too, and in time, she will understand that certain things are "NO!" Every time she approaches anything that is off limits—"NO!" But praise her highly when she is a good girl. Dogs learn what they can and what they can't do.

All of these words may seem discouraging, but just remember a puppy is a baby dog just like a human baby—she needs to be taught, she needs to learn and she needs to be protected. Your reward is a wonderful companion for all of the life of the Greyhound.

Are VCR tapes or remote controls stored at eye level? Pick up or put away anything that looks even remotely interesting. Start teaching family members to close closet doors, close doors to dog-restricted rooms, pick up dirty clothes and put away slippers. With a new dog or young puppy in the house, preventing problems from happening is very important.

If your Greyhound is going to have access to the garage, make sure all chemicals, paints and car parts are up high out of reach. Many things, like antifreeze, are very poisonous. You may even want to fence off part of the garage so there is absolutely no access to storage areas. By sectioning off the garage and picking up and storing away dangerous substances, you can ensure your dog's safety.

In the yard, look for possible escape routes, places where your dog could go under or over the fence. A pile of lumber or a rabbit hutch next to the fence could provide an easy escape route. A drainage ditch running under the fence could do the same thing. Again, just as in the house, try to look at your yard from the dog's point of view.

Puppies are naturally inquisitive and love to explore, so make sure your house has been thoroughly puppy-proofed.

PREPARING YOUR YARD

One final thing you may want to have before your Greyhound arrives is a fenced yard. If your yard is already fenced, you know how great it is to be able to open your door and let your dog exercise or relieve himself in safety. If you don't have one, contemplate how much easier it will be to housebreak your new dog. They can literally go out as many times as they need to, even in the middle of the night, and all you have to do is open the door. Besides, a fenced yard means that with people coming and going, if the dog scoots out, she won't be on the street but, rather, in the safety of her own yard.

Fences should never be shorter than 4 feet high, but preferably 5 feet. Most Greyhounds are not jumpers, but under the right emergency circumstances, many could leap 4 feet. This is an unlikely thing, but it is possible. If you have post and rail or board fencing, you will have to line it with wire so the dog does not get between the rails. Solid wood fencing is best of all because it provides a visible barrier, too.

Fence gates should be equipped with strong springs so that they automatically snap shut. Additionally, signs that remind people that there may be dogs in the yard are also a good idea. If possible, keep the gates locked as well. From time to time check the condition of your fencing. If the fence or the gates are in need of repair, do it immediately. Your dog's life might very well depend on it.

Also, safety check the yard. Put away garden tools, fertilizers, pesticides and pool supplies and remember to pick up potted plants before they become your dog's favorite play toys. Check your plants and landscaping to make sure they are safe for dogs just in case your Greyhound does try to sample them.

PREVENTION

Lots of problems with dogs can be avoided through simple prevention. Puppyproofing your home and yard is one way to keep your Greyhound safe and healthy.

Supervising the dog is another important means of prevention. If you are watching your Greyhound, she can't chew up your sofa. When you can't supervise her while she's in the house with you, put her in her crate or in the well-secured backyard. By supervising the dog, you can teach her what is allowed and what is not. Using the example of the sofa again, if your Greyhound puppy decides to take a nibble out of the sofa cushion and you are paying attention, you can tell the puppy, "Hey! No!" as she grabs the cushion. Then, you follow through by handing your puppy one of her chew toys and saying, "Here, chew on this instead." You have now prevented potential damage and, at the same time, taught your dog what she should chew.

TOYS FOR THE EX-RACER

Toys are the last items you need in your home before bringing home your Greyhound. Most ex-racers
are unfamiliar with toys, so they may need to be
introduced to them. Favorite toys include squeaky toys
of any variety. Those that are covered with fleece are
especially well-received. Not on the recommended
list are knotted ropes that you tug on one end while
your dog tugs on the other. This teaches all dogs, especially puppies, to use their mouths in an aggressive manner, and that is not something we ever want
them to do.

Plan Time to Bond

The last thing you need to do to prepare for the arrival
of your Greyhound is to plan to set aside a few days to
be at home with him. Take a few days off from work
and combine that with a weekend so you have the max-
imum amount of time possible. On the day the dog or
puppy comes home, do not, under any circumstances,
see this as an opportunity for a homecoming party. You
need to provide a safe, quiet atmosphere under which
your Greyhound can explore her new world and begin
to bond with you for life.

LOVE AND ATTENTION

Greyhounds are people-oriented dogs and need to
spend time with their owners. When you are home,
your dog should be inside with you and near your bed
at night. In addition, you will need to make time to
play with your dog, train her and make sure that she is
properly exercised.

If you think about it, you can come up with some cre-
ative ways to sneak in time with your Greyhound. To
spend time in the morning, getting up thirty minutes
earlier, will give you time for a fifteen- to twenty-minute
walk before taking your shower. If you work close to
home, your lunch hour might be just enough time
to get home and eat your lunch as you throw a ball

around for your dog. In the evening, take the children with you as you walk the dog; you can find out what's going on with the kids as you exercise and train your dog.

chapter 5

Feeding
Your
Greyhound

You can give your Greyhound all the love in the world, but if you aren't also feeding him the proper diet, he will not thrive. In fact, certain dietary deficiencies can produce severe results. Studies have shown, for example, that puppies fed a "Brand X" dog food versus those on a nutritionally complete variety experience stunted growth, among other things.

Getting Proper Nutrition

All dog food contains protein, fat, carbohydrates, vitamins, minerals and moisture in some combination. Knowing what each of these does for the body can help you understand why they must be fed in the proper proportions.

PROTEIN

Protein is considered crucial to growth of bones and muscle, the development of cell structures and strengthening the immune system. At different stages in a dog's life, different amounts of protein are needed. The younger the dog the more protein he needs. Older dogs generally need reduced levels of protein because it is hard on their kidneys.

FAT

Fat is an essential part of a dog's diet because it helps prevent dehydration and helps to boost the energy level. Oils are also necessary for a glossy coat. Again, more is needed in youth, less in old age.

CARBOHYDRATES

Carbohydrates are largely grain-based and make up the bulk of the content of dry kibble. Complex carbohydrates such as pasta or rice are digested slowly and provide energy for the dog's system on a time-release basis.

What Kind of Food?

Assessing the above we see that protein is necessary as a basis for growing and maintaining a dog, and fat gives a high energy boost whereas carbohydrates give a sustained energy boost. High quality commercial dog food is nutritionally complete, which means that the food has been balanced and analyzed for certain conditions. Puppy food will be high in protein and fat. Adult maintenance will be lower in protein and fat. Senior food will be lower still in protein and fat. Once your dog is off the track or the show circuit, there is no need to feed a high energy or so-called performance diet.

Many people develop an almost obsessive allegiance to one brand or another. Why this is so I cannot say but I do know this: There is no brand of dog food that is universally suited to all dogs. Just as some people prefer and even thrive on a particular diet, so do dogs. Some dogs have a beautiful sheen to their coat on a lamb and rice–based kibble. Other will develop gas from it. Some dogs crave a turkey and barley–based kibble while others won't touch it.

The best plan of action is trial and error. First find out what your dog has been eating and, if possible, get some of it. See how he does. If it agrees with him, stick to it. If, however, he develops gas, a dull coat, excessive amounts of stool or loose bowels, this is not the ideal food for him. Do not switch abruptly from one food to another. Make the change gradually by adding a proportion of the old with the new. After several weeks you should be able to tell if a particular brand is the right one for your dog or not.

A Racing Greyhound's Diet

Greyhounds at the track are fed a sort of stew consisting of raw meat, vegetables, vitamins and dry food. I find this to be an unsavory mixture in part because often the meat is what is known as 4-D, from cows that are dead, dying, diseased or down. Thanks, but no thanks. Besides, raw meat increases your dog's risk of salmonella or other types of food poisoning. So do not try to duplicate the track diet.

Keep It Interesting

Some people believe in feeding only dry food. Technically, and indeed scientifically, a dog can survive on it, but I feel that the addition of meat, vegetables and starch not only adds to the palatability of the food but also provides additional vitamins, minerals and a certain freshness that certainly is not seen in dry kibble. Besides, if you think about it, food is one of the few pleasures that a dog has. Why not make it nutritionally complete *and* tasty?

It is not very much trouble to add a little cooked meat to your dog's dry food. And, if you are cooking vegetables for your family, throw an extra carrot in the pot for the dog. A bit of the water that the vegetables were cooked in also adds to the flavor of the dog's meal when drizzled over his kibble.

Rice or pasta is always a welcome addition to the food bowl. Other accompaniments can include a few tablespoons of V-8 juice, a dollop of cottage cheese, a few teaspoons of fortified dried milk powder or a sprinkle of Parmesan cheese. Even a few heaping tablespoons of canned food well-mixed into the dry would not be amiss.

Remember I am not suggesting any of the above as a substitute for dry kibble. As long as your special additions do not make up more than 10 percent of your dog's diet, there is no chance they will throw off the nutritional balance of the kibble. But, these additions will definitely get an enthusiastic response from your dog plus they may actually be useful. Besides, since part of having a dog is about having fun, why not?

Vitamins and Minerals

If nutritionally complete foods are really complete, then why would anyone want to add supplements? Manufacturers of these foods would tell you that you don't have to. Manufacturers of supplements would tell you that you do. Nutritionally complete dog food is the canine equivalent of human food that has been analyzed and shown to have "X" amount of vitamins and minerals amounting to the recommended daily requirement (RDA). The RDA tends to be, to my way of thinking, on the low side. Yes, it will sustain life. Will it produce optimum health? Maybe.

Basically I think people fall into one of two categories: vitamin enthusiasts and non–vitamin enthusiasts. Dogs who live with either of those types will probably be on the same regimen as their owners. If you want to be absolutely sure your dog is getting every possible advantage, add supplements to his diet. Yes, there is a chance some of these added vitamins or minerals may be wasted by not being absorbed or perhaps not being needed to begin with. Others, however, just may provide an extra amount of a nutrient that your particular

dog is lacking or has a higher than average requirement for. Remember, just as no particular brand of dog
food is right for all dogs, not all dogs have *exactly* the
same need for nutrients. Dog foods are based on the
average dog and as we all know your dog is anything
but average!

How Much Should You Feed Your Greyhound?

Once you have chosen what to feed your dog, the next
consideration is how much to feed him. This is a little
tricky because what you are feeding him when he
comes to your home may not be what you should continue to feed him. Some ex-racers, for example, may
have been rescued from substandard conditions. In
that case, every effort must be made to fatten them up.
There is a limit to that, though, and some well-inten-
tioned owners continue to practically force-feed their
dogs long after their thin condition has disappeared.

*A well-fed, fit
Greyhound will
master agility
tricks with ease.*

Here is a sweeping generalization on how much to
feed a mature Greyhound, AKC or NGA: Average-sized
females (50 to 60 pounds) need approximately three
cups of dry and a half cup of canned per day total.
Average-sized males (65 to 75 pounds) need approximately four cups of dry and a half cup of canned per

day total. This is only a guideline, however. If your Greyhound is becoming too fat or too thin on those amounts, adjust accordingly. Likewise, if you choose not to add canned food, substitute an equal amount of dry.

I suggest you divide the amount you feed into two portions and give half in the morning and the other half at night. The reason is that it is easier on a dog's digestive tract not to have a huge quantity of food dumped on it all at once. It also gives the dog something to look forward to and allows him to eat at roughly the same time you do. By the way, do not get into the habit of feeding your dog little bits from your plate. It turns your dog into a beggar and allows him to dominate your meal. You don't beg for food from his bowl and he shouldn't do it from yours!

How Do I Feed My Greyhound?

Now that you know what you are going to feed and how much you are going to feed, the next question is "What are you going to put it in?" In a bowl, of course, but there are bowls and then there are bowls. I suggest you go for a stainless steel one. They are sanitary, can be put through the dishwasher and, if you happen to drop them, they won't break.

Greyhounds should be fed on an elevated surface, up at least 16 inches from the ground. Although Greyhounds are not particularly prone to the digestive disorder referred to as bloat (gastric torsion), it is not unknown in the breed either. An elevated dish lessens the dog's chances of getting bloat plus it is simply easier for them not to have to bend down so far.

Do not leave the dog's food out all day and allow him to nibble on it at will. Your Greyhound's food should be put out for him and taken up within ten minutes. After that, throw away what he didn't eat and wash the bowl. If you allow him to free feed the food can become rancid. And if you have more than one dog in the house, you'll never know who is eating and who isn't. Try the ten-minute test. After one or two times your dog will quickly figure out what meal time is all about.

FEEDING MORE THAN ONE DOG

Another note for homes with multiple dogs: Apart from the fact that if you free feed one dog may get it all while the other goes hungry, there is another thing to consider, namely, dog fights. Food is a real prize in the wild, and even domesticated dogs can become possessive over it.

If you have more than one dog, it is essential that you feed them separately and that you keep an eye on them while they are eating. It is not uncommon for one dog to inhale his food then wander over to the other dog's dish to see if he can beg a little extra. Many dogs,

A supply of fresh water should always be readily available for your dog.

even the most docile Greyhound, can become incensed by this and it wouldn't be long before a fight could break out.

Water

One thing that should always accompany food is water. In fact, fresh water should be available to your Greyhound at all times. If you are traveling, bring bottled water with you because a change in a dog's water can often bring on digestive upsets. Don't forget to scrub out the water bowl often, too.

Eating Something Undesirable

What if your Greyhound eats something he shouldn't? The something I'm referring to here is feces. Technically called copophragia, stool eating has unknown origins. Some people will tell you it is caused by a mineral deficiency. Others will tell you it is a nasty acquired habit. Regardless of the cause, there are a few things you can do about it.

First, keep your yard clean; this is an excellent idea anyway for many reasons. Second, there are products on the market that contain digestive enzymes that work to stop the habit. You add the powder to the dog's food and, supposedly, after a week to ten days, the problem should be over.

The final solution is a muzzle. For AKC Greyhounds, the device will be a foreign object and will take some getting used to, but for the NGA Greyhounds it's no different that putting on a collar. The best ones are plastic turnout muzzles equipped with a so-called stool cover that fastens on the end. The dog can still run around, do his business and, yes, breathe, but he will be unable to eat the unmentionable.

chapter 6

Grooming
Your
Greyhound

For some dogs, grooming is a labor intensive, complicated business. For the sleek Greyhound, however, it is neither. That doesn't mean that there is no work involved, just less of it.

Toenails

All of the weight of a dog is placed on her feet. At the tips of each of those toes are nails that grow. This may seem obvious but it is worth mentioning because many people neglect to trim their dog's toenails. There is no excuse for this. If you are either unwilling or unable to do it, for a few dollars you can take your dog to a groomer who will.

There is great discomfort caused to a dog with over-grown toenails. It makes it difficult for her to walk and can throw off the entire balance of the body if the poor dog is unable to make proper contact with the surface she is standing on. In extreme cases, the nails are so long that a dog must be anesthetized, the nails cut through the quick and then the tips cauterized. This is a costly and painful process that is easily avoided.

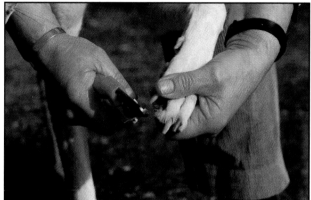

For your Grey-hound's comfort, trim her toenails every three weeks.

To prevent nails from becoming overgrown, they should be trimmed approximately every three weeks. Some dogs' nails grow faster, some slower. If you allow them to go more than a month without a trim, you've waited too long. At the track the dogs' nails are cut often, so with most Greyhounds a regular trimming is not a problem.

For dogs who are squeamish, the best bet is to have someone distract them while you, or a groomer, is trim-ming. Dangle a bit of ham in front of their nose, make funny noises or simply call their name. If they are truly intractable, a muzzle (again, the plastic turnout type) may be in order.

If you are going to do the trimming yourself, don't buy cheap nail clippers. The heavy duty, more expensive type make a cleaner cut and make the job much quicker. Cheap, dull blades invite accidents and often require numerous cuts before you are finished. Always keep at hand a bottle of styptic powder just in case you cut into the quick.

Coat Care

Although the coat of a Greyhound is short, this does not mean she never needs a bath. Her coat should be glossy, free of parasites and without odor. In general, Greyhounds do not have much, if any, doggy odor. When they do it means they are long overdue for a good shampoo.

BRUSHING

Brushing your Greyhound with a bristle (not nylon) hairbrush for a few minutes each day will help remove

loose hair and stimulate the follicles to produce the natural oils that give the coat its sheen. After you have finished giving your dog her daily brushing, carefully check her coat for any sores or trouble areas.

Brushing also gives you the opportunity to check for signs of flea or tick infestation. Ticks are large enough to be seen with the naked eye, especially if they are engorged with blood. Ticks carry disease and need to be removed immediately with a pair of tweezers or a hemostat. When you look for fleas, check for tiny black specks of feces, also known as "flea dirt." The most common place to find this clue is on the skin just forward of the tail, on the base of the spine.

Brush your Greyhound frequently with a bristle brush.

BATHING

How often you bathe your Greyhound depends in part on how active they are. Although dogs do not perspire the same way people do, they nonetheless get soiled from running, rolling in the grass, etc. Any extraneous material on your Greyhound's coat will eventually wind up on your furniture or carpet, so if for no other reason than that, you'll want to keep her clean.

Greyhounds need to be bathed more often in the summer than in the winter. A bath once a month in the warmer months will keep her coat healthy and smelling fresh. During the cooler months I generally give baths around Thanksgiving and not again until around the first of April.

While you are bathing your Greyhound, it is a good idea to check for fleas, ticks, lumps, sores or anything that shouldn't be there. Fleas and ticks will be discussed in detail in the next chapter, but if you are going to give your dog a flea bath (there is no tick bath), then make sure you use the mildest shampoo on the market for that purpose. A pyrethrin-based or d-Limonene–based flea shampoo will kill the fleas without hurting your dog. It is essential that you do not use a strong chemical dip or you could be jeopardizing your Greyhound's life!

Any sores or even more importantly lumps that you discover on your dog should be checked by your veterinarian. Early treatment could prevent a sore from becoming infected. In the case of lumps, it is good to know whether they are of the dangerous variety and, if they are, to get them taken care of before they become more serious.

EARS

Grooming is an ideal time to clean the ears.

While you are bathing your Greyhound, it is also a good time to clean your dog's ears. During the actual bath you should put cotton in their ears so water and shampoo do not drip down into the ear canal. After the bath, though, you should remove the cotton and,

using a cotton ball, wipe down as far into the ear as you can get. If there are excessive amounts of a black tarlike substance or if the inside of the ear is oozing, take your Greyhound to the vet. These could be the sign of ear mites or an infection. Just as is the case with every other medical condition, the sooner it is treated the better. Health problems rarely correct themselves without a little intervention.

Teeth

The final part of grooming involves the teeth. Since dogs cannot brush their own teeth we have to help them. If necessary, a deep cleaning can be performed under anesthesia by your vet. However, once the dog's teeth are really clean, it is up to you to maintain them. Giving your dog hard crunchy things to chew on helps keep her gums healthy. You can also brush your dog's teeth once a week or so with a specially designed toothbrush for dogs and specially flavored canine toothpaste. A gauze pad wrapped around your finger to rub across your dog's teeth helps prevent the build-up of tartar.

Make cleaning your Greyhound's teeth a priority for her overall health.

It is very important to make teeth cleaning a priority so you don't find your dog suffering from infected gums or abscessed teeth. Poor dental hygiene can lead to very serious complications such as bacteria from the dog's mouth lodging in the heart valve. Your dog can be left with a permanent disability from this and can even die. So, remember, keeping her teeth clean can also save her life!

chapter 7

Keeping Your Greyhound Healthy

Maintaining or achieving optimal health for your Greyhound should be the goal of every owner. In the last chapter we learned that proper feeding and grooming play an important role. In this chapter, we will discuss how to keep your dog fit, how to spot potential problems and how to prevent some easy-to-avoid hazards.

Having a healthy dog requires a lot more than a yearly checkup with the veterinarian. You will find, however, that most of the work is fun and allows you to develop an even closer bond with your dog.

Choosing a Veterinarian

Since a yearly veterinary checkup is an integral part of good care, let's start off with that. The first decision you have to make is who your veterinarian will be. Although your present vet may have served you well in the past, he or she may not be the best choice for your new Greyhound.

What you need to look for is a vet with sighthound experience. This person doesn't necessarily have to have treated Greyhounds, but he or she must be very familiar with one of the related breeds: Afghan Hounds, Borzoi or other sighthounds. The reason for that is that the anesthesia requirements and insecticide sensitivity of sighthounds are different from other kinds of dogs. One false step could kill your dog, so it is important that you choose your vet well. Be honest and ask your vet if he or she has other sighthounds as patients. If the answer is no or not many, you may want to consider someone else. Remember, this does not mean he or she is a bad vet, it just means that your Greyhound needs someone else.

Choose a veterinarian who has a lot of experience with sighthounds.

The breeder you bought your Greyhound from or the group you adopted your Greyhound from should be able to recommend a vet. If not, look through the Yellow Pages. Ask to speak to the vet on duty, ask how many sighthounds he or she sees in the practice and ask what type of anesthesia is used. The last is a key question—the ideal answer should be Isoflurane gas because it is tolerated well by most Greyhounds.

Apart from finding a vet who is familiar with sighthounds, you should also find one with whom you have a good rapport. He or she should be willing to answer all of your questions on all subjects of concern without exhibiting a condescending attitude or becoming offended. Your Greyhound should also be examined with gentleness and consideration. Remember, whomever you choose you may well have a relationship with for the next ten or twelve years. Be choosy: Your Greyhound is counting on you!

Anesthesia, De-wormers and Insecticides

You may be wondering why there is so much emphasis on anesthesia. The reason is that sighthounds react differently to anesthesia, and indeed many drugs, than do other dogs. As anesthesia leaves a dog's body, it is stored in the fat. Sighthounds have very little fat, so recovery for them is difficult. Additionally, the Greyhound's liver metabolizes drugs slower than that of other dogs, so drugs, too, must be administered with special care.

In addition to anesthesia itself presenting a problem, so, too, do the agents used to induce unconsciousness. Again, what works for most dogs is not appropriate for Greyhounds. Your vet should be aware of this difference and treat your Greyhound accordingly. In general, Valium or ketamine are safe for inducing unconsciousness, but it is necessary that you discuss this subject thoroughly with your vet.

Greyhounds' reactions to common de-wormers and insecticides are also different due to the reasons stated above. Most Greyhounds can be de-wormed of roundworm, hookworm and whipworm safely by use of Panacur. Tapeworm can be safely eradicated by the use of Droncit, either by tablet or injection.

Some people foolishly de-worm their dogs on a regular basis, some as often as once a month, without having any proof that the dog had worms! Do not fall into that trap. All de-wormers are a poison and present some degree of danger to your dog—especially if he never had worms to begin with. Remember the old adage: Poison the worm, not the dog.

The Examination

Even if your new Greyhound was recently examined by
the breeder's or the adoption group's veterinarian, it is
wise for your vet to examine him, too. This will give
him or her an opportunity to see your dog in what we
hope is peak condition.

KEEP RECORDS

One thing that you will need to bring to the examination is a copy of inoculation records (shots) and any
other health papers such as proof of spay/neuter or
the results of a heartworm test. These will be put in
your dog's permanent file. If your Greyhound is an ex-
racer and you were able to find out why he was retired,
that information should also be available.

Due to the nature of Greyhound rescue work, complete records on these dogs are not always made available to adoption groups. If a fecal test has not been
performed, you may want to bring along a stool sample
so it can be run through the machine and analyzed
while your dog is being examined.

A thorough examination will involve listening to your
dog's heart and lungs, looking in the eyes and ears and
looking down the throat. The teeth and gums will be
examined for signs of decay or gingivitis. Your dog will
also be palpated in the area of the abdomen and blad-
der to check for signs of any irregularities.

ABOUT WEIGHT

Your vet will also look at the overall condition of the
dog, including the condition of the coat and the
weight of the dog. For Greyhounds this is somewhat
tricky business because most people adopting ex-racers
get them at their racing weight. This is the equivalent
of adopting an athlete who has been involved in professional competitions. These dogs are extremely lean
with hardly any body fat, usually only 16 percent. It
is not necessary to keep them that lean. Thankfully,
most people are not guilty of underfeeding their
Greyhounds, but, unfortunately, many seriously over-
feed them.

Greyhounds are meant to be slim dogs. This does not mean emaciated or even at their racing weight. But their skeletal structure being what it is, too much weight puts a lot of stress on their joints.

Exercise is a great way to keep your Greyhound at his ideal weight.

Just as being overweight is unhealthy for people, it is unhealthy for dogs. Apart from the stress on skeletal structure, obesity has been associated with elevated blood sugar, heart problems, gastrointestinal disorders and respiratory problems.

How can you tell if your Greyhound is too fat? Give him this test: Put your thumbs on his backbone and your hands on his ribs. Can you feel the ribs easily? Then he is not too fat. If you have to do much feeling around, your Greyhound has a weight problem. It can be corrected either by reducing the amount of his food or by exercising him more.

Inoculations

Most inoculations are given on a yearly basis. Some protect only the dog's health. Others, however can also help prevent diseases such as rabies or leptospirosis, which are communicable to human beings. I say

YOUR PUPPY'S VACCINES

Vaccines are given to prevent your dog from getting an infectious disease like canine distemper or rabies. Vaccines are the ultimate preventive medicine: they're given before your dog ever gets the disease so as to protect him from the disease. That's why it is necessary for your dog to be vaccinated routinely. Puppy vaccines start at 8 weeks of age for the five-in-one DHLPP vaccine and are given every three to four weeks until the puppy is 16 months old. Your veterinarian will put your puppy on a proper schedule and will remind you when to bring in your dog for shots.

help prevent because most people do not realize that even a dog who is completely up-to-date on shots still has a small chance of picking up a disease. If vaccines were improperly administered to your dog when he was a puppy or if he has a weakened immune system, there is a greater chance that they will be less effective.

Regardless, you are greatly reducing his chances of being prey to disease if he is kept current. A list of the main inoculations that a dog needs yearly follows.

RABIES

This is a highly contagious virus usually carried by wildlife, especially bats, raccoons and skunks, although any warm-blooded animals, including humans, may become infected. The virus is transmitted through the saliva through a bite or break in the skin. The virus then travels up to the brain and spinal cord and throughout the body.

Behavioral changes are the first sign of the disease. Nocturnal animals, such as bats, will come out during the day, fearful or shy animals will become bold or aggressive or friendly and affectionate. (Raccoons, by the way, are not nocturnal animals, so just because you see one during the day do not assume it is rabid. But to be safe, do not touch it or any wild animal.) As the rabies virus spreads, the animal will have trouble swallowing and will drool or salivate excessively. Paralysis and convulsions are followed by death.

Stick to your puppy's vaccination schedule to help protect him from diseases.

DISTEMPER

Distemper is a very contagious viral disease that used to kill thousands of dogs. With the effective vaccines

73

available today, it should not kill any dogs, but, unfortunately, it still does.

Dogs with distemper are weak and depressed and have a discharge from the eyes and nose. Infected dogs cough, vomit and have diarrhea. Intravenous fluids and antibiotics may help support an infected dog, but, unfortunately, most die.

INFECTIOUS HEPATITUS

This is a highly contagious virus that primarily attacks the liver, but it can also cause severe kidney damage. It is not related to the form of hepatitis that affects people. The virus is spread through contaminated saliva, mucus, urine or feces. Initial symptoms include depression, vomiting, abdominal pain, high fever and jaundice.

Mild cases may be treated with intravenous fluids, antibiotics and even blood transfusions; however, the mortality rate is very high.

LEPTOSPIROSIS

Leptospirosis is a bacterial disease spread by the urine of infected wildlife. You might think that this is a hard disease for your dog to contract, but one taste of a bush that has been urinated on by infected wildlife, or one lap of contaminated water, is all it takes to become infected. This disease then attacks the kidneys and causes kidney failure.

Symptoms include fever, loss of appetite, possibly diarrhea and jaundice. Antibiotics can be used to treat the disease, but the outcome usually is not good due to the serious kidney and liver damage caused by the bacteria. Leptospirosis is highly contagious and can affect other dogs, animals and people.

PARVOVIRUS

Parvovirus, or parvo as it is commonly known, attacks the inner lining of the intestines, causing bloody diarrhea that has a distinct odor. It is a terrible killer of puppies and is extremely contagious. In puppies under 10 weeks of age, the virus also attacks the heart, causing death, often with no other symptoms. The virus moves rapidly, and dehydration can lead to shock and death in a matter of hours.

CANINE PARAINFLUENZA

Parainfluenza is a flu virus that affects the respiratory system of dogs. It can cause of variety of symptoms, including inflammation of the trachea, bronchi and lungs, as well as mild to severe coughing. Antibiotics may be prescribed to prevent or combat pneumonia, and a cough suppressant may quiet the cough. Luckily the majority of dogs recover quickly without any treatment.

BORDETELLA BRONCHISPECTICA

This respiratory virus, often called kennel cough, is airborne. Symptoms include sneezing, wheezing and a dry cough that may linger for weeks. The vaccine for this is administered through the nose (intranasally) by drops or a nasal spray.

CANINE CORONAVIRUS

As is implied by the name, this is also a virus. Coronavirus is rarely fatal to adult dogs, although it is frequently fatal to puppies. The symptoms include vomiting, loss of appetite and a yellowish, watery stool that might contain mucus or blood. The stools carry the shed virus, which is highly contagious. Fluid or electrolyte therapy can alleviate the dehydration associated with the diarrhea, but there is no treatment for the virus itself.

These, then, are the infectious diseases against which your dog can be inoculated. There are many other disorders, however, that cannot be prevented as easily. To familiarize yourself with the total picture of canine veterinary medicine, I recommend you purchase a copy of *The Dog Owner's Home Veterinary Handbook* by Delbert G. Carlson, D.V.M. and James M. Giffin, M.D.

(New York: Howell Book House, 1992). I recommend this book for purchase because it is something you should have in your home as a permanent reference.

Internal Parasites

While on the surface your Greyhound may appear healthy, he could be harboring internal parasites that can cause damage from sapping his strength to robbing him of nutrients and even killing him. For parasites lodged in the intestines, the only way to know for sure if he has any is by having your veterinarian perform a microscopic examination of a stool sample. It should be a fresh sample, but if you need to keep it overnight, it should be refrigerated. A tightly sealed jar should do the trick for storage. For the parasite that lives in the dog's heart, a blood sample must be drawn by a veterinarian.

ROUNDWORMS

Common internal parasites (l-r): roundworm, whipworm, tapeworm and hookworm.

These long white worms are commonly found internal parasites, especially in puppies, although they occasionally infest adult dogs and people. The adult female roundworm can lay up to 200,000 eggs a day, which are passed out in the dog's feces. Roundworms can only

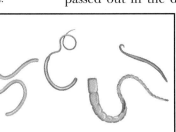

be transmitted via the feces. Because of this, stools should be picked up daily, and your dog should be prevented from investigating other dogs' feces.

If treated early, roundworms are not serious. However, a heavy infestation can severely affect a dog's health. Puppies with roundworms will not thrive and will become thin, with a dull coat and a pot-bellied appearance. In people, roundworms can be more serious; therefore, early treatment, regular fecal checks and good sanitation are important.

HOOKWORMS

Hookworms live their adult lives in the small intestines of dogs. They attach to the intestinal wall and suck blood. When they detach and move to a new location, the old wound continues to bleed because of the anticoagulant the worm injects when it bites. Because of this, bloody diarrhea is usually the first sign of a problem.

Hookworm eggs are passed through the feces. Either they are picked up from the stools, as with round-worms, or, if conditions are right, they hatch in the soil and attach themselves to the feet of their new hosts, where they can burrow into the skin. After burrowing through the skin, they migrate to the intestinal tract, where the cycle starts all over again.

People can pick up hookworms by walking barefoot in infected soil. In the Sunbelt states, children often pick up hookworm eggs when playing outside in the dirt or in a sandbox. Treatment for both dogs and people may have to be repeated.

TAPEWORMS

Tapeworms attach to the intestinal wall to absorb nutrients. They grow by creating new segments, and usually the first sign of an infestation is the ricelike segments found in the stools or on the dog's rectum. Tapeworms are acquired when a dog chews at a flea bite and swallows a flea, the intermediate host. Therefore, a good flea control program, which will be discussed later in this chapter, is the best way to prevent a tapeworm infestation.

WHIPWORMS

Adult whipworms live in the large intestine, where they feed on blood. The eggs are passed in the stool and can live in the soil for many years. If your dog eats the fresh spring grass or buries a bone in the yard, he can pick up eggs from the infected soil. If you garden, you can pick up eggs under your fingernails, infecting yourself if you touch your face.

Heavy infestations cause diarrhea, often watery or runny. The dog may appear thin or anemic with a poor coat. Severe bowel problems may result. Unfortunately, whipworms can be difficult to detect because the worms do not continually shed eggs. Therefore, a stool sample may be clear one day and the next day show eggs.

GIARDIA

Giardia is a protozoan which infects animals and people through contaminated water. Often the disease is asymptomatic, but it can produce bloody diarrhea. It is diagnosed by finding either the protozoan or cysts in the stool. You should prevent your dog from drinking water unless you know that it is safe.

HEARTWORM

Heartworm is spread by the bite of infected mosquitoes (the intermediate host), which are common, and spreading, in many parts of the country. Adult heartworms live in the upper heart and greater pulmonary arteries, where they severely damage the vessel walls. They are large worms and quickly clog the heart and pulmonary arteries. Poor circulation results, which in turn causes damage to other bodily functions; eventually death results from heart failure.

Many veterinarians recommend keeping dogs on heartworm preventative year-round because preventing heartworm is much easier than treating it. Before a dog begins taking preventative tablets, he must first test negative for the disease. Once-a-month heartworm tablets are safe for Greyhounds.

External Parasites
TICKS

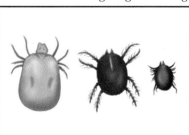

Three types of ticks (l-r): the wood tick, brown dog tick and deer tick.

While tick-borne diseases pose an ever-increasing risk for all dogs, ex-racers seem to be more at risk than most. This is not because they have a particular weakness, but because they often travel all over the country where they are exposed to all sorts of ticks and, sad to say, where not all receive the care they should.

The result is that an ex-racer from, say, Florida may wind up being placed in a home in New Jersey. And he may have brought with him ticks that he picked up while racing in Arizona. The adoption agency has probably bathed your dog and rid him of as many ticks as is humanly possible. Some tiny ticks are practically invisible while others can hide in unimaginable spots.

But, the damage that may have been done by the ticks may not be seen for some time to come. Some experts estimate that the number of racing Greyhounds who have been either exposed to tick diseases or who are actively sick from them is as high as 50 percent.

The most commonly seen tick-borne diseases are Lyme disease, Rocky Mountain spotted fever, babesiosis and Ehrlichiosis. All of these diseases can also be contracted by humans via ticks.

Luckily there are tests to determine if your dog has any of these diseases

Use tweezers to remove ticks from your dog.

and it is called a tick titer. A low reading may mean that your dog at some point in his life had been exposed to the disease or it may be the beginning of an active infection. Usually the presence of symptoms can help determine which is the case.

All of these diseases are treatable, but as with most things, the sooner the better. Antibiotics, usually doxycycline, are used to treat all but babesiosis. Babesiosis is treated by the use of a drug called Imidocarb, which requires that your vet get a special FDA license. Your adoption agency should be able to point you to a vet who has worked with this drug. If not, the tick-testing laboratory may be able to advise your vet on the proper protocol.

Tick diseases are not to be taken lightly. They can cause anything from paralysis to convulsions to death. Many dogs are misdiagnosed when what they really have is a tick disease. Get your dog tested for all of the above diseases.

FLEAS

The last of the external parasites is the flea, arch enemy of the dog. Until recently it was a constant battle during flea season to keep our dogs free of them. Now, thanks to some recent advances, no dog needs to suffer anymore.

A flea is a small insect about the size of a head of a pin. It is crescent-shaped, has six legs and is a tremendous jumper. Fleas live by biting the host animal and eating its blood.

You can see fleas by back-brushing the coat and looking at the skin. A flea will appear as a tiny darting speck, trying to hide in the hair. Fleas best show up on the dog's belly, near the genitals. You can also tell by having your dog lie on a solid colored sheet and brushing vigorously. If you see salt-and-pepper–type residue falling to the sheet, your Greyhound has fleas. The residue is made up of fecal matter (the "pepper") and eggs (the "salt").

A heavy infestation can actually kill a dog, especially the very young and very old. Keep in mind that each time a dog bites a flea, it eats a drop or two of blood. Multiply numerous bites a day by the number of fleas and you can see how dangerous an infestation can be.

Fleas biting their host can also cause other problems. Many Greyhounds are allergic to the flea's saliva and scratch each bite until a sore develops, which can become infected. This flea allergy, dermatitis, is a serious problem in many parts of the country. Fleas

FIGHTING FLEAS

Remember, the fleas you see on your dog are only part of the problem—the smallest part! To rid your dog and home of fleas, you need to treat your dog *and* your home. Here's how:

• Identify where your pet(s) sleep. These are "hot spots."

• Clean your pet's bedding regularly by vacuuming and washing.

• Spray "hot spots" with a non-toxic, long-lasting flea larvicide.

• Treat outdoor "hot spots" with insecticide.

• Kill eggs on pets with a product containing insect growth regulators (IGRs).

• Kill fleas on pets per your veterinarian's recommendation.

can also carry disease, such as the infamous bubonic plague, and are the intermediary host for tapeworms.

To reduce the flea population, you need to treat the dog and his environment. If you treat only the dog and not his house, yard and car, your Greyhound will simply become reinfected.

There are a number of flea-killing products on the market, but one new one that is safe for use on Greyhounds has all but made the others obsolete. It is called Advantage and it requires putting a few drops between the dog's shoulder blades and another few drops at the base of the tail. For a full month, any flea that jumps on your Greyhound will drop dead. The flea does not even have to bite, thus avoiding flea dermatitis. Nothing could be easier to use and this medication was tested on Greyhounds in its development.

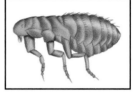

The flea is a die-hard pest.

Check for fleas while you give your dog a belly rub.

There is another new product called Front-line that kills both fleas and ticks and is effective longer, but it has disadvantages, too. While it is safe for use on Greyhounds, it requires that the flea actually bite the dog to work. This way the dog could still suffer from dermatitis. Additionally, it can take up to thirty-six hours to kill a tick and, by that time, the tick could have transmitted a disease.

For tick prevention I recommend good old-fashioned vigilance, perhaps coupled with a collar containing Amitraz. It is safe for use on Greyhounds and it repels ticks. The only drawback is that the collars themselves are hazardous to Greyhounds if they eat one or even if they play-bite the neck of a dog wearing one, so keep that in mind before deciding whether to use one.

If you want to give your dog a flea bath, then you must avoid any shampoos containing organophosphates or carbamates. Your Greyhound can be literally poisoned by these on the spot. Stick tape labeled "BAD BAD BAD" on any products that are hazardous to your dog as a reminder.

First Aid and Emergencies

Certain problems require administering first aid to your dog. The following advice is not comprehensive and is not a substitute for veterinary care. Do what you can to stabilize your dog, then contact your veterinarian.

COMMON FIRST SITUATIONS

Your Greyhound can't tell you when something's wrong with him. But if you spend enough time with your dog, you'll know intuitively when he's not feeling well. When you notice that he is not acting in his usual way, ask yourself these questions:

- What made you think there was a problem?

- What was the first clue that something was wrong?

- Is your Greyhound eating normally?

- Does your Greyhound have a temperature? (Continue reading for instructions on taking your dog's temperature.)

- What do his stools look like?

- Is your Greyhound limping?

- When you do a hands-on exam, is he sore anywhere? Can you feel a lump? Is anything red or swollen?

Keep a written record of everything you've noticed. When you call your veterinarian, be ready to give specific details about your Greyhound's condition.

IN AN EMERGENCY

When you visit your veterinarian for the first time, ask for an emergency number to call. This is essential to have if something happens to your Greyhound during non-regular working hours. Keep this number posted by the phone so you don't have to frantically search for it when a real emergency hits. Make a practice trip to the emergency clinic so you will know exactly where to go without any confusion. You'll need to be as calm as possible in a real emergency, and knowing how long it will take to get to the clinic is important.

Fever When you call your veterinarian, he or she will ask whether your dog has a fever. Using a rectal thermometer (the kind used for people) you can **take your dog's temperature**. A dog's normal temperature is between 101 and 102 degrees Fahrenheit. Shake the thermometer down and put some petroleum jelly on the tip. If possible, ask for someone to assist you by holding your Greyhound at his head so that he can't squirm around too much. Lift up your dog's tail and insert the thermometer into the anus about one inch. Don't let go of it! Keep holding the thermometer and watch your clock. After three minutes, withdraw the thermometer, wipe it off and read the temperature.

A FIRST-AID KIT

Keep a canine first-aid kit on hand for general care and emergencies. Check it periodically to make sure liquids haven't spilled or dried up, and replace medications and materials after they're used. Your kit should include:

Activated charcoal tablets

Adhesive tape
(1 and 2 inches wide)

Antibacterial ointment
(for skin and eyes)

Aspirin (buffered or enteric coated, *not* Ibuprofen)

Bandages: Gauze rolls
(1 and 2 inches wide)
and dressing pads

Cotton balls

Diarrhea medicine

Dosing syringe

Hydrogen peroxide (3%)

Petroleum jelly

Rectal thermometer

Rubber gloves

Rubbing alcohol

Scissors

Tourniquet

Towel

Tweezers

Vomiting Your veterinarian will also ask whether your dog is vomiting. He or she will also ask what the vomit looked like. Is it regurgitated food (which never makes it further than the esophagus and looks like slime-covered food) or vomit (digested food)? Was there anything unusual in it, like plant remnants or garbage or glass? Did your dog vomit once or several times?

Unusual Bowel Movements You will be asked similar questions about the dog's bowel movements. Did the dog have a bowel movement? If so, did it look normal? Was there blood or mucus in the stool? Did the stool smell different or peculiar? Did you see any foreign objects in the stool?

Your veterinarian will most likely want to see your Greyhound. Your answers to these questions will help your veterinarian form an early diagnosis of your Greyhound's problem and will prepare him or her for what to expect when you come in.

WHEN TO CALL THE VET

In any emergency situation, you should call your veterinarian immediately. You can make the difference in your dog's life by staying as calm as possible when you call and by giving the doctor or the assistant as much information as possible before you leave for the clinic. That way, the vet will be able to take immediate, specific action to remedy your dog's situation.

Emergencies include acute abdominal pain, suspected poisoning, snakebite, burns, frostbite, shock, dehydration, abnormal vomiting or bleeding, and deep wounds. You are the best judge of your dog's health, as you live with and observe him every day. Don't hesitate to call your veterinarian if you suspect trouble.

There are situations that you'll need to handle to some extent yourself before you bring your Greyhound to the veterinarian.

Use a scarf or old hose to make a temporary muzzle.

Animal Bites If another dog or animal bites your Greyhound and he's in pain, you'll need to put a temporary muzzle on him. That way you can touch the area of the wound without getting bitten or snapped at. To make the muzzle, use a pair of panty hose or a long piece of gauze. Wrap it around the dog's muzzle, cross it under the jaw and then pull it around the dog's head, tying it back.

Trim the hair from around the wound and pour hydrogen peroxide liberally over it. A handheld pressure bandage can help stop the bleeding. If the bite is a rip or tear, stitches may be necessary. Your veterinarian may also recommend putting the dog on antibiotics. Make sure the other animal was not rapid. If you can't be sure but suspect it was, inform your veterinarian immediately.

Bee Stings   Many dogs are allergic to bee stings. If your Greyhound is, you'll know immediately because the sting will start to swell. Take your dog to the veterinarian immediately for a treatment of antihistamine.

Bleeding   Muzzle your dog if he is in pain. Place a gauze pad or a clean

Run your hands regularly over your dog to feel for any injuries.

cloth over the wound and apply pressure to stop the bleeding. If the bleeding doesn't stop or if the wound will require stitches, call your veterinarian. If the wound is on a leg and continues to bleed, apply a tourniquet, but make sure it is loosened every fifteen minutes. Take your dog to the veterinarian as soon as possible.

Choking   If your Greyhound is pawing at his mouth, coughing, gagging or drooling, he may have something caught in his mouth or throat. Open his jaws and shine a flashlight down his throat. If you can see the object, reach in and pull it out, using your fingers, tweezers or a pair of pliers. If you cannot see anything and your dog is still choking, hit him behind the neck between the shoulders to try and dislodge the object. If this fails, use an adapted Heimlich maneuver or abdominal thrust. For the Heimlich maneuver, with your dog standing, grasp either side of the rib cage and squeeze. Be careful with his ribs, but try to make a sharp enough movement to cause the air in the lungs to force the object out. For the abdominal thrust, lay your dog on his side and, using your palms together, press in quick, sharp motions just behind the rib cage.

*Applying ab-
dominal thrusts
can save a
choking dog.*

If your Greyhound can breathe around the object, take him to the veterinarian immediately. If your dog cannot breathe around the object, you don't have time to move him. Keep working on getting the object dislodged.

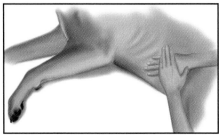

Diarrhea Diarrhea is characterized by loose, watery stools that can be caused by many things. (Severe diarrhea that is accompanied by straining and bloody stools is called colitis.) From something as simple as eating something he shouldn't, like spoiled food from the garbage, another animal's feces or plants, your dog can have a bout of diarrhea. Once the offending matter has passed, the diarrhea goes away. Feeding your dog small meals of a bland diet such as boiled meat and plain rice can help him feel better. Most importantly, make sure that your dog has access to plenty of water (diarrhea is extremely dehydrating). You can also give your dog an antidiarrheal medicine such as Loperamide. If you don't see improvement or the diarrhea looks particularly bad, contact your veterinarian immediately.

*Make a temporary
splint by wrap-
ping the leg in
firm casing, then
bandaging it.*

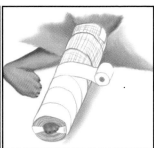

Fractures Because a broken bone causes great pain, muzzle your Greyhound immediately if you suspect he has this injury. Try to immobilize the limb in a temporary splint by using a piece of wood and then wrapping it with gauze or soft cloth. If you can use a door or board as a backboard or stretcher so that the injured limb stays stable, use it. Transport the dog to the veterinarian as soon as possible.

Broken Nails   A ripped or broken toenail can be extremely painful. If your dog is frantic, muzzle him to protect yourself. If a piece of the nail is hanging, trim it off, then pour hydrogen peroxide over the nail. If the nail is bleeding, run it over a soft bar of soap; the soap will help the nail clot. If the quick of the nail is showing or if the nail has broken off under the skin, call your veterinarian; antibiotics might be needed to prevent an infection.

Overheating or Heatstroke   If your Greyhound is too hot and has difficulty breathing, starts panting rapidly, vomits or collapses, you need to take action immediately. These are all symptoms of heatstroke, which can be life-threatening. Immediately place your Greyhound in a tub of cool water (not freezing cold water) or, if a tub is not available, run water from a hose over your dog. Encourage your dog to drink some cool water. Take his temperature and call your veterinarian right away.

Poisoning   Many products and plants can be toxic to your Greyhound. Antifreeze is one such product, and dogs are attracted to it because it tastes sweet. Insecticides, paints, household chemicals and various plants are all dangerous to curious dogs, especially those inquisitive puppies!

A number of houseplants, including avocado, dieffenbachia, English Ivy, jasmine, philodendron, and the bulbs of the amaryllis, daffodil, hyacinth, narcissus, iris, and tulip are poisonous. So are apple seeds, cherry pits, chocolate, mushrooms, peaches, rhubarb, tobacco and walnuts. At Christmas, be sure your dog does not ingest holly or mistletoe berries. Whatever marijauna

Some of the many household substances harmful to your dog.

and jimson weed may do to your own health, they are definitely toxic to your dog.

When your dog is outside in your yard, do not let eat andromeda, arrowgrass, azalea, bittersweet, boxwood, buttercups, caladium, castor beans, choke-cherry, climbing lily, crown of thorns, daphne, delphinium, dieffenbachia, dumb cane, elephant ear, elderberry, foxglove, hemlock, hydrangea, laburnum, larkspur, laurel, locoweed, marigold, monkshood, nightshade, oleander, poison ivy, privet, rhododendron, snow on the mountain, stinging nettle, toadstools, wisteria and yew.

Symptoms of poisoning include retching and vomiting, diarrhea, salivation, labored breathing, dilated pupils, weakness, collapse or convulsions. Sometimes one or more symptoms will show, depending on the poison. Timing is critical if you suspect your dog has ingested a poison. Call your veterinarian right away. If you can't get in touch with your veterinarian, contact the National Animal Poison Control Center hot line (1-800-548-2423). The hotline and your veterinarian can better treat your dog if you can tell them what and approximately how much was ingested. *Do not make your dog vomit unless instructed to do so!*

Giving Your Greyhound Medicine

Some medications can be surprisingly easy to administer; some can be difficult. Some dogs don't mind having ointment put in their eyes or taking a pill; others

Squeeze eye ointment into the lower lid.

resist. Have your veterinarian share some pointers with you and follow these instructions.

To **administer eye ointment** in the eye without poking the dog with the tube, stand behind your dog and cuddle his head up against your legs. Using one hand, gently pull the lower eyelid slightly away from the eye. At the same time, squeeze some of the ointment into the lower eyelid. When the dog closes his eye, the medication will be distributed over the eye.

There are a couple of different techniques to **give your dog a pill**. The easiest way is to keep a jar of baby food on hand. Dip the pill in it and your Greyhound should eagerly lick the pill (covered with baby food) right from your hand. Some dogs are tricky and will lick the food and spit out the pill, so you'll need to be more careful. Have your Greyhound sit, then stand behind him straddling his back. With the pill in one hand, pull your dog's head up and back gently so that his muzzle is pointing up. Open his mouth and very swiftly drop the pill in at the back of his throat. Close his mouth and massage his throat until he swallows. Before you let him go, open his mouth and check to see whether the pill's gone. Follow up the medicine with a treat.

You can give **liquid medication** the same way, pouring it into your dog's mouth. You want to make sure that your Greyhound doesn't inhale the medication instead of swallowing it. An easy way to measure the medicine is to use a chicken or turkey baster or a large eye-drop-per. Put the tip of the baster into the dog's mouth from the side (between the molars) and, holding the dog's mouth shut, squeeze the medication in while you tilt his head backward slightly so that the medicine runs into, instead of out of, the mouth.

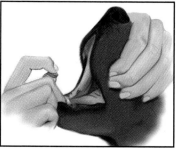

To give a pill, open the mouth wide, then drop it in the back of the throat.

Applying **skin ointments** is usually easy. Simply part the hair so that you're putting the ointment directly on the skin, and rub it in according to the directions. Keeping your Greyhound from licking the ointment can be another story, and licking often makes the problem worse. If your dog has a bad skin condition or stitches that need to heal, your veterinarian will probably give you an Elizabethan collar for him. This large plastic collar, named for the fashion styles during the reign of Queen Elizabeth I, extends at least to the tip of your dog's nose. The collar is unattractive and clumsy, and most dogs absolutely hate it, but it's the only way the wound will have a chance to heal.

Don't be afraid to ask your veterinarian questions when he or she prescribes medication or treatments for your

Greyhound. It is important that you understand what the drug(s) is, what it does, if it has side effects and how long your dog should take it. Make sure that you understand what your dog's problem is, what the course of treatment will do, and what you should (or should not) expect. With that knowledge, be sure to follow through on the course of treatment. If your veterinarian rec-

An Elizabethan collar keeps your dog from licking a fresh wound.

ommends that you give the medication for ten days, give it for ten days; don't stop at five days just because your dog looks better. Again, if you have any problems or reservations, call your veterinarian.

Spaying and Neutering

There are more reasons you should consider spaying or neutering your pet Greyhound than you probably think. If you own a pet Greyhound or are currently trying to locate one, you are probably interested only in the companionship aspect of the breed. And that's just what you should be interested in. Your female Greyhound does not have to have a canine family to be fulfilled; she has a human one. You are the center of her universe, and she doesn't need anything or anyone else. If you have your Greyhound female spayed at the proper time, she will never get the urge to mate and she won't miss it.

The advantages of spaying or neutering your Greyhound are many. Not only does the operation preclude any accidental matings, but there are also considerable health benefits.

Females who have been spayed are unable to contract pyometra, an infection of the uterus that is common in unspayed females. The risk of mammary tumors is also greatly diminished. For males, testicular and prostate cancer are eliminated.

Spayed or neutered pets have a more even temperament since they are not subject to the strong instinct to breed. Unneutered males can become aggressive if they are prevented from getting to a female in season. They are more likely to jump a fence or dart out the door if they catch the scent of a female in heat.

If you have your male Greyhound neutered, he will be better able to focus on being the family pet than the frustrated lothario. He will not have the urge to roam in search of potential mates and will probably be cleaner at home.

When unspayed females go into heat, they often are subject to mood swings due to fluctuating hormones. This could make an otherwise placid dog irritable. Many females bleed for a full three weeks, making it difficult to keep your dog and your house clean.

In addition, you must keep a *very* careful watch on her all the time, and make sure no males have access to her. Suitors can become quite aggressivein their pursuits and may mark your home to show their territory.

Equally compelling is the fact you know you will not have been responsible for bringing even more

---

ADVANTAGES OF SPAY/NEUTER

The greatest advantage of spaying (for females) or neutering (for males) your dog is that you are guaranteed your dog will not produce puppies. There are too many puppies already available for too few homes. There are other advantages as well.

ADVANTAGES OF SPAYING

No messy heats.

No "suitors" howling at your windows or waiting in your yard.

Decreased incidences of pyometra (disease of the uterus) and breast cancer.

ADVANTAGES OF NEUTERING

Lessens male aggressive and territorial behaviors, but doesn't affect the dog's personality. Behaviors are often owner-induced, so neutering is not the only answer, but it is a good start.

Prevents the need to roam in search of bitches in season.

Decreased incidences of urogenital diseases.

---

dogs into this world. While the case is different for the AKC Greyhound, the NGA Greyhounds are still being put to sleep at the rate of about 20,000 a year.

If your Greyhound was of breeding quality, he would not have ended up in an adoption program. And, even if he is the most beautiful and the most athletic, there are thousands more out there just as great. Instead of breeding your ex-racer, spay or neuter, then adopt another dog who might otherwise have been put to death by someone not so caring as you.

As Your Greyhound Ages

To live a long life in good health, your Greyhound will need your help. Like people, dogs encounter changes and problems as they age. Your Greyhound's vision will dim, his hearing will fade and his joints will stiffen. Heart and kidney disease are common in older dogs. Reflexes will not be as sharp as they once were, and your Greyhound's sensitivity to heat and cold will become more acute. Your dog's temperament may change, showing less tolerance to younger dogs, children and other things that are not part of his set routine.

Having an old dog who has lived his life with you is a special gift. Your old Greyhound knows your ways, your likes and dislikes and your habits. Sometimes you may even think he can read your mind, and you can sense that his greatest joy is just being close to you. Your old Greyhound may not be able to do the work that he did when he was younger, but he can still be a wonderful companion.

Arthritis   Arthritis is common in old dogs. The joints get stiff, especially when the weather is cool. Your Greyhound may need assistance getting up in the morning. Make sure that you add some soft and warm padding to your Greyhound's beds, not just for sleeping, but all day. Talk to your veterinarian about treatment; there are pain relievers that can help.

Nutrition   Your dog will need to consume fewer calories and less protein as his activity level slows down and his body ages. Some old dogs have an additional problem with food digestion that can be noticed by poor stools and a dull coat. Several dog food manufacturers offer easily digested, premium-quality foods for senior dogs.

Exercise   Your old Greyhound still needs the stimulation of exercise. Being able to walk around is good for the circulation and seeing and smelling the world is a healthy mental diversion. A leisurely walk around the neighborhood might be just enough.

When It's Time

There will come a time when you sense that your dog is suffering more that he needs to, and you will have to decide how to relieve his pain. Only you can make the decision, but spare your companion the humiliation of incontinence, convulsions or the inability to stand up or move around. Your veterinarian can advise you on the condition of your dog, but don't let him or her make this decision for you.

When you know it's time, call your veterinarian. He or she can give your dog a tranquilizer, then an injection that is an overdose of an anesthetic. Your already sleepy dog will quietly stop breathing. Be there with your dog. Give your dog the comfort of your soothing voice and tell him how much you love him as he goes to sleep in your arms. There will be no fear, and the last thing your dog will remember is your love.

GRIEVING

A well-loved dog is an emotional investment of unparalleled returns. Unfortunately, our dogs' lives are entirely too short and we must learn to cope with inevitably losing them. When you lose a loved one, whether it is a pet, spouse, friend or family member, it is natural to grieve. The intensity and duration of grief is different for every person and for each loss.

Sometimes the best way to deal with grief is with a good hard cry. For others, talking about their pet is good therapy. Talking to others who have lost an old dog and can relate to your loss can be especially helpful. You may want to bury your old friend in a special spot where you can go to remember the times you shared together. You could also ask your veterinarian about having your dog cremated and keeping his ashes in a special urn in your home.

Another Greyhound

If yours was a one-Greyhound household, you will probably want another to fill the empty space left by your old friend. The time to seek a new dog is for you to determine, but it is better to let a little time go by. This way, you give yourself a chance to heal from the loss of your old pet, and allow the newcomer to make her way to your heart in her own way.

Your Happy, Healthy Pet

Your Dog's Name _____

Name on Your Dog's Pedigree (if your dog has one) _____

_____

Where Your Dog Came From _____

_____

Your Dog's Birthday _____

Your Dog's Veterinarian

    Name _____

    Address _____

    Phone Number_____

    Emergency Number_____

Your Dog's Health

    Vaccines

    type _____ date given _____

    type _____ date given _____

    type _____ date given _____

    type _____ date given _____

    Heartworm

    date tested _____ type used_____ start date _____

Your Dog's License Number_____

Groomer's Name and Number _____

Dogsitter/Walker's Name and Number_____

Awards Your Dog Has Won

    Award _____ date earned _____

    Award _____ date earned _____

part three

Enjoying
your
Dog

chapter 8

Basic
Training

by Ian Dunbar, Ph.D., MRCVS

Training is the jewel in the crown—the most important aspect of doggy husbandry. There is no more important variable influencing dog behavior and temperament than the dog's education: A well-trained, well-behaved and good-natured puppydog is always a joy to live with, but an untrained and uncivilized dog can be a perpetual nightmare. Moreover, deny the dog an education and it will not have the opportunity to fulfill its own canine potential; neither will it have the ability to communicate effectively with its human companions.

Luckily, modern psychological training methods are easy, efficient and effective and, above all, considerably dog-friendly and user-friendly. Doggy education is as simple as it is enjoyable. But before

98

you can have a good time play-training with your new dog, you have to learn what to do and how to do it. There is no bigger variable influencing the success of dog training than the *owner's* experience and expertise. *Before you embark on the dog's education, you must first educate yourself.*

Basic Training for Owners

Ideally, basic owner training should begin well *before* you select your dog. Find out all you can about your chosen breed first, then master rudimentary training and handling skills. If you already have your puppy/dog, owner training is a dire emergency—the clock is running! Especially for puppies, the first few weeks at home are the most important and influential days in the dog's life. Indeed, the cause of most adolescent and adult problems may be traced back to the initial days the pup explores his new home. This is the time to establish the *status quo*—to teach the puppy/dog how you would like him to behave and so prevent otherwise quite predictable problems.

In addition to consulting breeders and breed books such as this one (which understandably have a positive breed bias), seek out as many pet owners with your breed you can find. Good points are obvious. What you want to find out are the breed-specific *problems*, so you can nip them in the bud. In particular, you should talk to owners with *adolescent* dogs and make a list of all anticipated problems. Most important, *test drive* at least half a dozen adolescent and adult dogs of your breed yourself. An eight-week-old puppy is deceptively easy to handle, but she will acquire adult size, speed and strength in just four months, so you should learn now what to prepare for.

Puppy and pet dog training classes offer a convenient venue to locate pet owners and observe dogs in action. For a list of suitable trainers in your area, contact the Association of Pet Dog Trainers (see Chapter 13). You may also begin your basic owner training by observing other owners in class. Watch as many classes and test drive as many dogs as possible. Select an upbeat, dog-friendly, people-friendly, fun-and-games, puppydog pet training class to learn the ropes. Also, watch training videos and read training books (see Chapter 12). You must find out what to do and how to do it *before* you have to do it.

Principles of Training

Most people think training comprises teaching the dog to do things such as sit, speak and roll over, but even a four-week-old pup knows how to do these things already. Instead, the first step in training involves teaching the dog human words for each dog behavior and activity and for each aspect of the dog's environment. That way you, the owner, can more easily participate in the dog's domestic education by directing him to perform specific actions appropriately, that is, at the right time, in the right place, and so on. Training opens communication channels, enabling an educated dog to at least understand the owner's requests.

In addition to teaching a dog *what* we want her to do, it is also necessary to teach her *why* she should do what we ask. Indeed, 95 percent of training revolves around motivating the dog *to want to do* what we want. Dogs often understand what their owners want; they just don't see the point of doing it—especially when the owner's repetitively boring and seemingly senseless instructions are totally at odds with much more pressing and exciting doggy distractions. It is not so much the dog who is being stubborn or dominant; rather, it is the owner who has failed to acknowledge the dog's needs and feelings and to approach training from the dog's point of view.

The Meaning of Instructions

The secret to successful training is learning how to use training lures to predict or prompt specific behaviors—to coax the dog to do what you want *when* you want. Any highly valued object (such as a treat or toy) may be used as a lure, which the dog will follow with his eyes and nose. Moving the lure in specific ways entices the dog to move his nose, head and entire body in specific ways. In fact, by learning the art of manipulating various lures, it is possible to teach the dog to assume virtually any body position and perform any action. Once you have control over the expression of the dog's behaviors and can elicit any body position or behavior at will, you can easily teach the dog to perform on request.

Tell your dog what you want him to do, use a lure to entice him to respond correctly, then profusely praise

Teach your dog words for each activity he needs to know, like down.

and maybe reward him once he performs the desired action. For example, verbally request "Fido, sit!" while you move a squeaky toy upwards and backwards over the dog's muzzle (lure-movement and hand signal), smile knowingly as he looks up (to follow the lure) and sits down (as a result of canine anatomical engineering), then praise him to distraction ("Gooood Fido!"). Squeak the toy, offer a training treat and give your dog and yourself a pat on the back.

Being able to elicit desired responses over and over enables the owner to reward the dog over and over. Consequently, the dog begins to think training is fun. For example, the more the dog is rewarded for sitting, the more she enjoys sitting. Eventually the dog comes to realize that, whereas most sitting is appreciated, sitting immediately upon request usually prompts especially enthusiastic praise and a slew of high-level rewards. The dog begins to sit on cue much of the time, showing that she is starting to grasp the meaning of the owner's verbal request and hand signal.

Why Comply?

Most dogs enjoy initial lure/reward training and are only too happy to comply with their owners' wishes. Unfortunately, repetitive drilling without appreciative feedback tends to diminish the dog's enthusiasm until he eventually fails to see the point of complying anymore. Moreover, as the dog approaches adolescence he becomes more easily distracted as he develops other interests. Lengthy sessions with repetitive exercises tend to bore and demotivate both parties. If it's not fun, the owner doesn't do it and neither does the dog.

Integrate training into your dog's life: The greater number of training sessions each day and the *shorter* they are, the more willingly compliant your dog will become. Make sure to have a short (just a few seconds) training interlude before every enjoyable canine activity. For example, ask your dog to sit to greet people, to sit before you throw his Frisbee, and to sit for his supper. Really, sitting is no different from a canine "please." Also, include numerous short training interludes during every enjoyable canine pastime, for example, when playing with the dog or when he is running in the park. In this fashion, doggy distractions may be effectively converted into rewards for training. Just as all games have rules, fun becomes training . . . and training becomes fun.

Eventually, rewards actually become unnecessary to continue motivating your dog. If trained with consideration and kindness, performing the desired behaviors will become self-rewarding and, in a sense, your dog will motivate himself. Just as it is not necessary to reward a human companion during an enjoyable walk in the park, or following a game of tennis, it is hardly necessary to reward our best friend—the dog—for walking by our side or while playing fetch. Human company during enjoyable activities is reward enough for most dogs.

Even though your dog has become self-motivating, it's still good to praise and pet him a lot and offer rewards once in a while, especially for a good job well done. And if for no other reason, praising and rewarding others is good for the human heart.

To train your dog, you need gentle hands, a loving heart and a good attitude.

Punishment

Without a doubt, lure/reward training is by far the best way to teach: Entice your dog to do what you want and then reward him for doing so. Unfortunately, a human shortcoming is to take the good for granted and to moan and groan at the bad. Specifically, the dog's many good behaviors are ignored while the owner focuses on punishing the dog for making mistakes. In extreme cases, instruction is *limited* to punishing mistakes made by a trainee dog, child, employee or husband, even though it has been proven punishment training is notoriously inefficient and ineffective and is decidedly unfriendly and combative. It teaches the dog that training is a drag, almost as quickly as it teaches the dog to dislike his trainer. Why treat our best friends like our worst enemies?

Punishment training is also much more laborious and time consuming. Whereas it takes only a finite amount of time to teach a dog what to chew, for example, it takes much, much longer to punish the dog for each and every mistake. Remember, *there is only one right way!* So why not teach that right way from the outset?!

To make matters worse, punishment training causes severe lapses in the dog's reliability. Since it is obviously impossible to punish the dog each and every time she misbehaves, the dog quickly learns to distinguish between those times when she must comply (so as to avoid impending punishment) and those times when she need not comply, because punishment is impossible. Such times include when the dog is off leash and only six feet away, when the owner is otherwise engaged (talking to a friend, watching television, taking a shower, tending to the baby or chatting on the telephone), or when the dog is left at home alone.

Instances of misbehavior will be numerous when the owner is away, because even when the dog complied in the owner's looming presence, he did so unwillingly. The dog was forced to act against his will, rather than moulding his will to want to please. Hence, when the owner is absent, not only does the dog know he need not comply, he simply does not want to. Again, the trainee is not a stubborn vindictive beast, but rather the trainer has failed to teach.

Punishment training invariably creates unpredictable Jekyll and Hyde behavior.

Trainer's Tools

Many training books extol the virtues of a vast array of training paraphernalia and electronic and metallic gizmos, most of which are designed for canine restraint, correction and punishment, rather than for actual facilitation of doggy education. In reality, most effective training tools are not found in stores; they come from within ourselves. In addition to a willing dog, all you really need is a functional human brain, gentle hands, a loving heart and a good attitude.

In terms of equipment, all dogs do require a quality buckle collar to sport dog tags and to attach the leash (for safety and to comply with local leash laws). Hollow chewtoys (like Kongs or sterilized longbones) and a dog bed or collapsible crate are a must for housetraining. Three additional tools are required:

1. specific lures (training treats and toys) to predict and prompt specific desired behaviors;

2. rewards (praise, affection, training treats and toys) to reinforce for the dog what a lot of fun it all is; and

3. knowledge—how to convert the dog's favorite activities and games (potential distractions to training) into "life-rewards," which may be employed to facilitate training.

The most powerful of these is *knowledge*. Education is the key! Watch training classes, participate in training classes, watch videos, read books, enjoy playtraining with your dog, and then your dog will say "Please," and your dog will say "Thank you!"

Housetraining

If dogs were left to their own devices, certainly they would chew, dig and bark for entertainment and then no doubt highlight a few areas of their living space with sprinkles of urine, in much the same way we decorate by hanging pictures. Consequently, when we ask a dog to live with us, we must teach him *where* he may dig and perform his toilet duties, *what* he may chew and *when* he may bark. After all, when left at home alone for many hours, we cannot expect the dog to amuse himself by completing crosswords or watching the soaps on TV!

Also, it would be decidedly unfair to keep the house rules a secret from the dog, and then get angry and punish the poor critter for inevitably transgressing rules he did not even know existed. Remember, without adequate education and guidance, the dog will be forced to establish his own rules—doggy rules—that most probably will be at odds with the owner's view of domestic living.

Since most problems develop during the first few days the dog is at home, prospective dog owners must be certain they are quite clear about the principles of housetraining *before* they get a dog. Early misbehaviors quickly become established as the status quo—

becoming firmly entrenched as hard-to-break bad habits, which set the precedent for years to come. Make sure to teach your dog good habits right from the start. Good habits are just as hard to break as bad ones!

Ideally, when a new dog comes home, try to arrange for someone to be present for as much as possible during the first few days (for adult dogs) or weeks for puppies. With only a little forethought, it is surprisingly easy to find a puppy sitter, such as a retired person, who would be willing to eat from your refrigerator and watch your television while keeping an eye on the newcomer to encourage the dog to play with chewtoys and to ensure he goes outside on a regular basis.

POTTY TRAINING

To teach the dog where to relieve himself:

1. never let him make a single mistake;

2. let him know where you want him to go; and

3. handsomely reward him for doing so: "GOOOOOOOD DOG!!!" liver treat, liver treat, liver treat!

PREVENTING MISTAKES

A single mistake is a training disaster, since it heralds many more in future weeks. And each time the dog soils the house, this further reinforces the dog's unfortunate preference for an indoor, carpeted toilet. *Do not let an unhousetrained dog have full run of the house if you are away from home or cannot pay full attention.* Instead, confine the dog to an area where elimination is appropriate, such as an outdoor run or, better still, a small, comfortable indoor kennel with access to an outdoor run. When confined in this manner, most dogs will naturally housetrain themselves.

If that's not possible, confine the dog to an area, such as a utility room, kitchen, basement or garage, where elimination may not be desired in the long run but as an interim measure it is certainly preferable to doing it all around the house. Use newspaper to cover the floor of the dog's day room. The newspaper may be used to soak up the urine and to wrap up and dispose of the feces. Once your dog develops a preferred spot for eliminating, it is only necessary to cover that part of the floor with newspaper. The smaller papered area may then be moved (only a little each day) towards the door to the outside. Thus the dog will develop the tendency to go to the door when he needs to relieve himself.

Never confine an unhousetrained dog to a crate for long periods. Doing so would force the dog to soil the crate and ruin its usefulness as an aid for housetraining (see the following discussion).

The first few weeks at home are the most important and influential in your dog's life.

TEACHING WHERE

In order to teach your dog where you would like her to do her business, you have to be there to direct the proceedings—an obvious, yet often neglected, fact of life. In order to be there to teach the dog *where* to go, you need to know *when* she needs to go. Indeed, the success of housetraining depends on the owner's ability to predict these times. Certainly, a regular feeding schedule will facilitate prediction somewhat, but there is nothing like "loading the deck" and influencing the timing of the outcome yourself!

Whenever you are at home, make sure the dog is under constant supervision and/or confined to a small area. If already well trained, simply instruct the dog to lie down in his bed or basket. Alternatively, confine the dog to a crate (doggy den) or tie-down (a short, 18-inch lead that can be clipped to an eye hook in the baseboard). Short-term close confinement strongly inhibits urination and defecation, since the dog does not want to soil his sleeping area. Thus, when you release the puppydog each hour, he will definitely need to urinate immediately and defecate every third or fourth hour. Keep the dog confined to his doggy den and take him to his intended toilet area each hour, every hour, and on the hour.

When taking your dog outside, instruct him to sit quietly before opening the door—he will soon learn to sit by the door when he needs to go out!

TEACHING WHY

Being able to predict when the dog needs to go enables the owner to be on the spot to praise and reward the dog. Each hour, hurry the dog to the intended toilet area in the yard, issue the appropriate instruction ("Go pee!" or "Go poop!"), then give the dog three to four minutes to produce. Praise and offer a couple of training treats when successful. The treats are important because many people fail to praise their dogs with feeling . . . and housetraining is hardly the time for understatement. So either loosen up and enthusiastically praise that dog: "Wuzzzer-wuzzer-wuzzer, hoooser good wuffer den? Hoooo went pee for Daddy?" Or say "Good dog!" as best you can and offer the treats for effect.

Following elimination is an ideal time for a spot of playtraining in the yard or house. Also, an empty dog may be allowed greater freedom around the house for the next half hour or so, just as long as you keep an eye out to make sure he does not get into other kinds of mischief. If you are preoccupied and cannot pay full attention, confine the dog to his doggy den once more to enjoy a peaceful snooze or to play with his many chewtoys.

If your dog does not eliminate within the allotted time outside—no biggie! Back to his doggy den, and then try again after another hour.

As I own large dogs, I always feel more relaxed walking an empty dog, knowing that I will not need to finish our stroll weighted down with bags of feces! Beware of falling into the trap of walking the dog to get it to eliminate. The good ol' dog walk is such an enormous highlight in the dog's life that it represents the single biggest potential reward in domestic dogdom. However, when in a hurry, or during inclement weather, many owners abruptly terminate the walk the moment the dog has done its business. This, in effect, severely punishes the dog for doing the right thing, in the right place at the right time. Consequently, many dogs become strongly inhibited from eliminating outdoors because they know it will signal an abrupt end to an otherwise thoroughly enjoyable walk.

Instead, instruct the dog to relieve himself in the yard prior to going for a walk. If you follow the above instructions, most dogs soon learn to eliminate on cue. As soon as the dog eliminates, praise (and offer a treat or two)—"Good dog! Let's go walkies!" Use the walk as a reward for eliminating in the yard. If the dog does not go, put him back in his doggy den and think about a walk later on. You will find with a "No feces–no walk" policy, your dog will become one of the fastest defecators in the business.

If you do not have a back yard, instruct the dog to eliminate right outside your front door prior to the walk. Not only will this facilitate clean up and disposal of the feces in your own trash can but, also, the walk may again be used as a colossal reward.

CHEWING AND BARKING

Short-term close confinement also teaches the dog that occasional quiet moments are a reality of domestic living. Your puppydog is extremely impressionable during his first few weeks at home. Regular confinement at this time soon exerts a calming influence over the dog's personality. Remember, once the dog is housetrained and calmer, there will be a whole lifetime ahead for the dog to enjoy full run of the house and garden. On the other hand, by letting the newcomer have unrestricted access to the entire household and allowing him to run willy-nilly, he will most certainly develop a bunch of behavior problems in short order, no doubt necessitating confinement later in life. It would not be fair to remedially restrain and confine a dog you have trained, through neglect, to run free.

When confining the dog, make sure he always has an impressive array of suitable chewtoys. Kongs and sterilized longbones (both readily available from pet stores) make the best chewtoys, since they are hollow and may be stuffed with treats to heighten the dog's interest. For example, by stuffing the little hole at the top of a Kong with a small piece of freeze-dried liver, the dog will not want to leave it alone.

Remember, treats do not have to be junk food and they certainly should not represent extra calories. Rather, treats should be part of each dog's regular daily diet:

Make sure your puppy has suitable chewtoys.

Some food may be served in the dog's bowl for breakfast and dinner, some food may be used as training treats, and some food may be used for stuffing chewtoys. I regularly stuff my dogs' many Kongs with different shaped biscuits and kibble. The kibble seems to fall out fairly easily, as do the oval-shaped biscuits, thus rewarding the dog instantaneously for checking out the chewtoys. The bone-shaped biscuits fall out after a while, rewarding the dog for worrying at the chewtoy. But the triangular biscuits never come out. They remain inside the Kong as lures, maintaining the dog's fascination with its chewtoy. To further focus the dog's interest, I always make sure to flavor the triangular biscuits by rubbing them with a little cheese or freeze-dried liver.

If stuffed chewtoys are reserved especially for times the dog is confined, the puppy-dog will soon learn to enjoy quiet moments in her doggy den and she will quickly develop a chewtoy habit—a good habit! This is a simple *passive training* process; all the owner has to do is set up the situation and the dog all but trains herself—easy and effective. Even when the dog is given run of the house, her first inclination will be to indulge her rewarding chewtoy habit rather than destroying less-attractive household articles, such as curtains, carpets, chairs and compact disks. Similarly, a chewtoy chewer will be less inclined to scratch and chew herself excessively. Also, if the dog busies herself as a recreational chewer, she will be less inclined to develop into a recreational barker or digger when left at home alone.

Stuff a number of chewtoys whenever the dog is left confined and remove the extra-special-tasting treats when you return. Your dog will now amuse himself with his chewtoys before falling asleep and then resume playing with his chewtoys when he expects you to return. Since most owner-absent misbehavior happens right after you leave and right before your expected return, your puppydog will now be conveniently preoccupied with his chewtoys at these times.

To teach come, call your dog, open your arms as a welcoming signal, wave a toy or a treat and praise for every step in your direction.

Come and Sit

Most puppies will happily approach virtually anyone, whether called or not; that is, until they collide with adolescence and develop other more important doggy interests, such as sniffing a multiplicity of exquisite odors on the grass. Your mission, Mr. and/or Ms. Owner, is to teach and reward the pup for coming reliably, willingly and happily when called—and you have just three months to get it done. Unless adequately reinforced, your puppy's tendency to approach people will self-destruct by adolescence.

Call your dog ("Fido, come!"), open your arms (and maybe squat down) as a welcoming signal, waggle a treat or toy as a lure, and reward the puppydog when he comes running. Do not wait to praise the dog until he reaches you—he may come 95 percent of the way and then run off after some distraction. Instead, praise the dog's *first* step towards you and continue praising enthusiastically for *every* step he takes in your direction.

When the rapidly approaching puppy dog is three lengths away from impact, instruct him to sit ("Fido, sit!") and hold the lure in front of you in an outstretched hand to prevent him from hitting you mid-chest and knocking you flat on your back! As Fido decelerates to nose the lure, move the treat upwards and backwards just over his muzzle with an upwards motion of your extended arm (palm-upwards). As the dog looks up to follow the lure, he will sit down (if he jumps up, you are holding the lure too high). Praise the dog for sitting. Move backwards and call him again. Repeat this many times over, always praising when Fido comes and sits; on occasion, reward him.

For the first couple of trials, use a training treat both as a lure to entice the dog to come and sit and as a reward for doing so. Thereafter, try to use different items as lures and rewards. For example, lure the dog with a Kong or Frisbee but reward her with a food treat. Or lure the dog with a food treat but pat her and throw a tennis ball as a reward. After just a few repetitions, dispense with the lures and rewards; the dog will begin to respond willingly to your verbal requests and hand signals just for the prospect of praise from your heart and affection from your hands.

Instruct every family member, friend and visitor how to get the dog to come and sit. Invite people over for a series of pooch parties; do not keep the pup a secret— let other people enjoy this puppy, and let the pup enjoy other people. Puppydog parties are not only fun, they easily attract a lot of people to help *you* train *your* dog. Unless you teach your dog *how* to meet people, that is, to sit for greetings, no doubt the dog will resort to jumping up. Then you and the visitors will get annoyed, and the dog will be punished. This is not fair. *Send out those invitations for puppy parties and teach your dog to be mannerly and socially acceptable.*

Even though your dog quickly masters obedient recalls in the house, his reliability may falter when playing in the back yard or local park. Ironically, it is *the owner* who has unintentionally trained the dog *not* to respond in these instances. By allowing the dog to play and run around and otherwise have a good time, but then to call the dog to put him on leash to take him home, the dog quickly learns playing is fun but training is a drag. Thus, playing in the park becomes a severe distraction, which works against training. Bad news!

Instead, whether playing with the dog off leash or on leash, request him to come at frequent intervals— say, every minute or so. On most occasions, praise and pet the dog for a few seconds while he is sitting, then tell him to go play again. For especially fast recalls, offer a couple of training treats and take the time to praise and pet the dog enthusiastically before releasing him. The dog will learn that coming when called is not necessarily the end of the play session, and neither is it the end of the world; rather, it signals an enjoyable, quality time-out with the owner before resuming play once more. In fact, playing in the park now becomes a very effective life-reward, which works to facilitate training by reinforcing each obedient and timely recall. Good news!

Sit, Down, Stand and Rollover

Teaching the dog a variety of body positions is easy for owner and dog, impressive for spectators and extremely useful for all. Using lure-reward techniques, it is possible to train several positions at once to verbal commands or hand signals (which impress the socks off onlookers).

Sit and *down*—the two control commands—prevent or resolve nearly a hundred behavior problems. For example, if the dog happily and obediently sits or lies down when requested, he cannot jump on visitors, dash out the front door, run around and chase its tail, pester other dogs, harass cats or annoy family, friends or strangers. Additionally, "sit" or "down" are better emergency commands for off-leash control.

It is easier to teach and maintain a reliable sit than maintain a reliable recall. *Sit* is the purest and simplest of commands—either the dog is sitting or he is not. If there is any change of circumstances or potential danger in the park, for example, simply instruct the dog to sit. If he sits, you have a number of options: allow the dog to resume playing when he is safe; walk up and put the dog on leash, or call the dog. The dog will be much more likely to come when called if he has already acknowledged his compliance by sitting. If the dog does not sit in the park—train him to!

Stand and *rollover-stay* are the two positions for examining the dog. Your veterinarian will love you to distraction if you take a little time to teach the dog to stand still and roll over and play possum. Also, your vet bills will be smaller. The rollover-stay is an especially useful command and is really just a variation of the down-stay: whereas the dog lies prone in the traditional down, she lies supine in the rollover-stay.

As with teaching come and sit, the training techniques to teach the dog to assume all other body positions on cue are user-friendly and dog-friendly. Simply give the appropriate request, lure the dog into the desired body position using a training treat or toy and then *praise* (and maybe reward) the dog as soon as he complies. Try not to touch the dog to get him to respond. If you teach the dog by guiding him into position, the dog will quickly learn that rump-pressure means sit, for example, but as yet you still have no control over your dog if he is just six feet away. It will still be necessary to teach the dog to sit on request. So do not make training a time-consuming two-step process; instead, teach the dog to sit to a verbal request or hand signal from the outset. Once the dog sits willingly when requested, by all means use your hands to pet the dog when he does so.

To teach *down* when the dog is already sitting, say "Fido, down!," hold the lure in one hand (palm down) and lower that hand to the floor between the dog's forepaws. As the dog lowers his head to follow the lure, slowly move the lure away from the dog just a fraction (in front of his paws). The dog will lie down as he stretches his nose forward to follow the lure. Praise the dog when he does so. If the dog stands up, you pulled the lure away too far and too quickly.

When teaching the dog to lie down from the standing position, say "down" and lower the lure to the floor as before. Once the dog has lowered his forequarters and assumed a play bow, gently and slowly move the lure *towards* the dog between his forelegs. Praise the dog as soon as his rear end plops down.

After just a couple of trials it will be possible to alternate sits and downs and have the dog energetically perform doggy push-ups. Praise the dog a lot, and after half a dozen or so push-ups reward the dog with a training treat or toy. You will notice the more energetically you move your arm—upwards (palm up) to get the dog to sit, and downwards (palm down) to get the dog to lie down—the more energetically the dog responds to your requests. Now try training the dog in silence and you will notice he has also learned to respond to hand signals. Yeah! Not too shabby for the first session.

To teach *stand* from the sitting position, say "Fido, stand," slowly move the lure half a dog-length away from the dog's nose, keeping it at nose level, and praise the dog as he stands to follow the lure. As soon

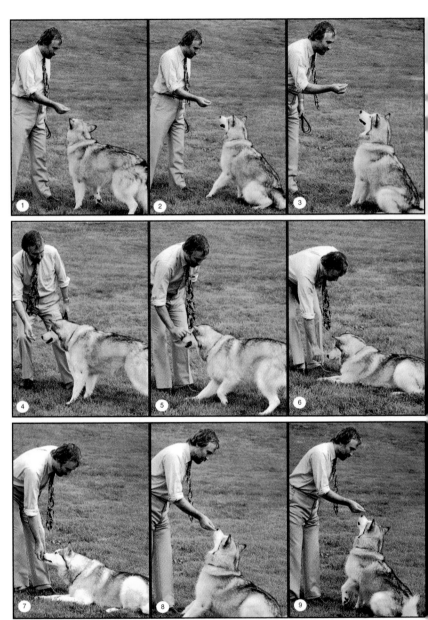

Using a food lure to teach sit, down and stand. 1) "Phoenix, Sit." 2) Hand palm upwards, move lure up and back over dog's muzzle. 3) "Good sit, Phoenix!" 4) "Phoenix, down." 5) Hand palm downwards, move lure down to lie between dog's forepaws. 6) "Phoenix, off. Good down, Phoenix!" 7) "Phoenix, sit!" 8) Palm upwards, move lure up and back, keeping it close to dog's muzzle. 9) "Good sit, Phoenix!"

10) "Phoenix, stand!" 11) Move lure away from dog at nose height, then lower it a tad. 12) "Phoenix, off! Good stand, Phoenix!" 13) "Phoenix, down!" 14) Hand palm downwards, move lure down to lie between dog's forepaws. 15) "Phoenix, off! Good down-stay, Phoenix!" 16) "Phoenix, stand!" 17) Move lure away from dog's muzzle up to nose height. 18) "Phoenix,off! Good stand-stay, Phoenix. Now we'll make the vet and groomer happy!"

as the dog stands, lower the lure to just beneath the dog's chin to entice him to look down; otherwise he will stand and then sit immediately. To prompt the dog to stand from the down position, move the lure half a dog-length upwards and away from the dog, holding the lure at standing nose height from the floor.

Teaching **rollover** is best started from the down position, with the dog lying on one side, or at least with both hind legs stretched out on the same side. Say "Fido, bang!" and move the lure backwards and alongside the dog's muzzle to its elbow (on the side of its outstretched hind legs). Once the dog looks to the side and backwards, very slowly move the lure upwards to the dog's shoulder and backbone. Tickling the dog in the goolies (groin area) often invokes a reflex-raising of the hind leg as an appeasement gesture, which facilitates the tendency to roll over. If you move the lure too quickly and the dog jumps into the standing position, have patience and start again. As soon as the dog rolls onto its back, keep the lure stationary and mesmerize the dog with a relaxing tummy rub.

To teach **rollover-stay** when the dog is standing or moving, say "Fido, bang!" and give the appropriate hand signal (with index finger pointed and thumb cocked in true Sam Spade fashion), then in one fluid movement lure him to first lie down and then rollover-stay as above.

Teaching the dog to **stay** in each of the above four positions becomes a piece of cake after first teaching the dog not to worry at the toy or treat training lure. This is best accomplished by hand feeding dinner kibble. Hold a piece of kibble firmly in your hand and softly instruct "Off!" Ignore any licking and slobbering *for however long the dog worries at the treat*, but say "Take it!" and offer the kibble *the instant* the dog breaks contact with his muzzle. Repeat this a few times, and then up the ante and insist the dog remove his muzzle for one whole second before offering the kibble. Then progressively refine your criteria and have the dog not touch your hand (or treat) for longer and longer periods on each trial, such as for two seconds, four seconds, then six, ten, fifteen, twenty, thirty seconds and so on. The dog soon learns: (1) worrying at the treat never gets results, whereas (2) noncontact is often rewarded after a variable time lapse.

Teaching *"Off!"* has many useful applications in its own right. Additionally, instructing the dog not to touch a training lure often produces spontaneous and magical stays. Request the dog to stand-stay, for example, and not to touch the lure. At first set your sights on a short two-second stay before rewarding the dog. (Remember, every long journey begins with a single step.) However, on subsequent trials, gradually and progressively increase the length of stay required to receive a reward. In no time at all your dog will stand calmly for a minute or so.

Relevancy Training

Once you have taught the dog what you expect her to do when requested to come, sit, lie down, stand, rollover and stay, the time is right to teach the dog *why* she should comply with your wishes. The secret is to have many (*many*) extremely short training interludes (two to five seconds each) at numerous (*numerous*) times during the course of the dog's day. Especially work with the dog immediately *before* the dog's good times and *during* the dog's good times. For example, ask your dog to sit and/or lie down each time before opening doors, serving meals, offering treats and tummy rubs; ask the dog to perform a few controlled doggy push-ups before letting her off-leash or throwing a tennis ball; and perhaps request the dog to sit-down-sit-stand-down-stand-rollover before inviting her to cuddle on the couch.

Similarly, request the dog to sit many times during play or on walks, and in no time at all the dog will be only too pleased to follow your instructions because he has learned that a compliant response heralds all sorts of goodies. Basically all you are trying to teach the dog is how to say please: "Please throw the tennis ball. Please may I snuggle on the couch."

Remember, whereas it is important to keep training interludes short, it is equally important to have many short sessions each and every day. The shortest (and most useful) session comprises asking the dog to sit and then go play during a play session. When trained this way, your dog will soon associate training with good times. In fact, the dog may be unable to distinguish between training and good times and, indeed, there should be no distinction. The warped concept that training involves forcing the dog to comply and/or dominating his will is totally at odds with the picture of a truly well-trained dog. In reality, enjoying a game of training with a dog is no different from enjoying a game of backgammon or tennis with a friend; and walking with a dog should be no different from strolling with buddies on the golf course.

Walk by Your Side

Many people attempt to teach a dog to heel by putting him on a leash and physically correcting the dog when he makes mistakes. There are a number of things seriously wrong with this approach, the first being that most people do not want precision heeling; rather, they simply want the dog to follow or walk by their side. Second, when physically restrained during "training," even though the dog may grudgingly mope by your side when "handcuffed" on leash, let's see what happens when he is off leash. History! The dog is in the next county because he never enjoyed walking with you on leash and you have no control over him off leash. So let's just teach the dog off leash from the outset to *want* to walk with us. Third, if the dog has not been trained to heel, it is a trifle hasty to think about punishing the poor dog for making mistakes and breaking heeling rules he didn't even know existed. This is simply not fair! Surely, if the dog had been adequately taught how to heel, he would seldom make mistakes and hence there would be no need to correct the dog. Remember, each mistake and each correction (punishment) advertise the trainer's inadequacy, not the dog's. The dog is not stubborn, he is not stupid and he is not bad. Even if he were, he would still require training, so let's train him properly.

Let's teach the dog to *enjoy* following us and to *want* to walk by our side offleash. Then it will be easier to teach high-precision off-leash heeling patterns if desired. After attaching the leash for safety on outdoor walks, but before going anywhere, it is necessary to teach the dog specifically not to pull. Now it will be much easier to teach on-leash walking and heeling because the dog already wants to walk with you, he is familiar with the desired walking and heeling positions and he knows not to pull.

FOLLOWING

Start by training your dog to follow you. Many puppies will follow if you simply walk away from them and maybe click your fingers or chuckle. Adult dogs may require additional enticement to stimulate them to follow, such as a training lure or, at the very least, a lively trainer. To teach the dog to follow: (1) keep walking and (2) walk away from the dog. If the dog attempts to lead or lag, change pace; slow down if the dog forges too far ahead, but speed up if he lags too far behind. Say "Steady!" or "Easy!" each time before you slow down and "Quickly!" or "Hustle!" each time before you speed up, and the dog will learn to change pace on cue. If the dog lags or leads too far, or if he wanders right or left, simply walk quickly in the opposite direction and maybe even run away from the dog and hide.

Practicing is a lot of fun; you can set up a course in your home, yard or park to do this. Indoors, entice the dog to follow upstairs, into a bedroom, into the bathroom, downstairs, around the living room couch, zigzagging between dining room chairs and into the kitchen for dinner. Outdoors, get the dog to follow around park benches, trees, shrubs and along walkways and lines in the grass. (For safety outdoors, it is advisable to attach a long line on the dog, but never exert corrective tension on the line.)

Remember, following has a lot to do with attitude—*your* attitude! Most probably your dog will *not* want to follow Mr. Grumpy Troll with the personality of wilted lettuce. Lighten up—walk with a jaunty step, whistle a happy tune, sing, skip and tell jokes to your dog and he will be right there by your side.

By Your Side

It is smart to train the dog to walk close on one side or the other—either side will do, your choice. When walking, jogging or cycling, it is generally bad news to have the dog suddenly cut in front of you. In fact, I train my dogs to walk "By my side" and "Other side"—both very useful instructions. It is possible to position the dog fairly accurately by looking to the appropriate side and clicking your fingers or slapping your thigh on that side. A precise positioning may be attained by holding a training lure, such as a chewtoy, tennis ball, or food treat. Stop and stand still several times throughout the walk, just as you would when window shopping or meeting a friend. Use the lure to make sure the dog slows down and stays close whenever you stop.

When teaching the dog to heel, we generally want her to sit in heel position when we stop. Teach heel

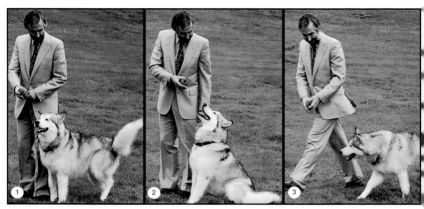

Using a toy to teach sit-heel-sit sequences: 1) "Phoenix, heel!" Standing still, move lure up and back over dog's muzzle…. 2) To position dog sitting in heel position on your left side. 3) "Phoenix, heel!" wagging lure in left hand. Change lure to right hand in preparation for sit signal.

position at the standstill and the dog will learn that the default heel position is sitting by your side (left or right—your choice, unless you wish to compete in obedience trials, in which case the dog must heel on the left).

Several times a day, stand up and call your dog to come and sit in heel position—"Fido, heel!" For example, instruct the dog to come to heel each time there are commercials on TV, or each time you turn a page of a novel, and the dog will get it in a single evening.

Practice straight-line heeling and turns separately. With the dog sitting at heel, teach him to turn in place. After each quarter-turn, half-turn or full turn in place, lure the dog to sit at heel. Now it's time for short straight-line heeling sequences, no more than a few steps at a time. Always think of heeling in terms of Sit-Heel-Sit sequences—start and end with the dog in position and do your best to keep him there when moving. Progressively increase the number of steps in each sequence. When the dog remains close for 20 yards of straight-line heeling, it is time to add a few turns and then sign up for a happy-heeling obedience class to get some advice from the experts.

4) Use hand signal only to lure dog to sit as you stop. Eventually, dog will sit automatically at heel whenever you stop. 5) "Good dog!"

NO PULLING ON LEASH

You can start teaching your dog not to pull on leash anywhere—in front of the television or outdoors—but regardless of location, you must not take a single step with tension in the leash. For a reason known only to dogs, even just a couple of paces of pulling on leash is intrinsically motivating and diabolically rewarding. Instead, attach the leash to the dog's collar, grasp the other end firmly with both hands held close to your chest, and stand still—do not budge an inch. Have somebody watch you with a stopwatch to time your progress, or else you will never believe this will work and so you will not even try the exercise, and your shoulder and the dog's neck will be traumatized for years to come.

Stand still and wait for the dog to stop pulling, and to sit and/or lie down. All dogs stop pulling and sit eventually. Most take only a couple of minutes; the all-time record is 22 $\frac{1}{5}$ minutes. Time how long it takes. Gently praise the dog when he stops pulling, and as soon as he sits, enthusiastically praise the dog and take just one step forwards, then immediately stand still. This single step usually demonstrates the ballistic reinforcing nature of pulling on leash; most dogs explode to the end of the leash, so be prepared for the strain. Stand firm and wait for the dog to sit again. Repeat this half a dozen times and you will probably notice a progressive reduction in the force of the dog's one-step explosions and a radical reduction in the time it takes for the dog to sit each time.

As the dog learns "Sit we go" and "Pull we stop," she will begin to walk forward calmly with each single step and automatically sit when you stop. Now try two steps before you stop. Wooooooo! Scary! When the dog has mastered two steps at a time, try for three. After each success, progressively increase the number of steps in the sequence: try four steps and then six, eight, ten and twenty steps before stopping. Congratulations! You are now walking the dog on leash.

Whenever walking with the dog (off leash or on leash), make sure you stop periodically to practice a few position commands and stays before instructing the dog to "Walk on!" (Remember, you want the dog to be compliant everywhere, not just in the kitchen when his dinner is at hand.) For example, stopping every 25 yards to briefly train the dog amounts to over 200 training interludes within a single three-mile stroll. And each training session is in a different location. You will not believe the improvement within just the first mile of the first walk.

To put it another way, integrating training into a walk offers 200 separate opportunities to use the continuance of the walk as a reward to reinforce the dog's education. Moreover, some training interludes may comprise continuing education for the dog's walking skills: Alternate short periods of the dog walking calmly by your side with periods when the dog is allowed to sniff and investigate the environment. Now sniffing odors on the grass and meeting other dogs become rewards which reinforce the dog's calm and mannerly demeanor. Good Lord! Whatever next? Many enjoyable walks together of course. Happy trails!

THE IMPORTANCE OF TRICKS

Nothing will improve a dog's quality of life better than having a few tricks under its belt. Teaching any trick expands the dog's vocabulary, which facilitates communication and improves the owner's control. Also, specific tricks help prevent and resolve specific behavior problems. For example, by teaching the dog to fetch his toys, the dog learns carrying a toy makes the owner happy and, therefore, will be more likely to chew his toy than other inappropriate items.

More important, teaching tricks prompts owners to lighten up and train with a sunny disposition. Really, tricks should be no different from any other behaviors we put on cue. But they are. When teaching tricks, owners have a much sweeter attitude, which in turn motivates the dog and improves her willingness to comply. The dog feels tricks are a blast, but formal commands are a drag. In fact, tricks are so enjoyable, they may be used as rewards in training by asking the dog to come, sit and down-stay and then rollover for a tummy rub. Go on, try it: Crack a smile and even giggle when the dog promptly and willingly lies down and stays.

Most important, performing tricks prompts onlookers to smile and giggle. Many people are scared of dogs, especially large ones. And nothing can be more off-putting for a dog than to be constantly confronted by strangers who don't like him because of his size or the way he looks. Uneasy people put the dog on edge, causing him to back off and bark, only frightening people all the more. And so a vicious circle develops, with the people's fear fueling the dog's fear *and vice versa*. Instead, tie a pink ribbon to your dog's collar and practice all sorts of tricks on walks and in the park, and you will be pleasantly amazed how it changes people's attitudes toward your friendly dog. The dog's repertoire of tricks is limited only by the trainer's imagination. Below I have described three of my favorites:

SPEAK AND SHUSH

The training sequence involved in teaching a dog to bark on request is no different from that used when training any behavior on cue: request—lure—response—reward. As always, the secret of success lies in finding an effective lure. If the dog always barks at the doorbell, for example, say "Rover, speak!", have an accomplice ring the doorbell, then reward the dog for barking. After a few woofs, ask Rover to "Shush!", waggle a food treat under his nose (to entice him to sniff and thus to shush), praise him when quiet and eventually offer the treat as a reward. Alternate "Speak" and "Shush," progressively increasing the length of shush-time between each barking bout.

PLAYBOW

With the dog standing, say "Bow!" and lower the food lure (palm upwards) to rest between the dog's forepaws. Praise as the dog lowers her forequarters and sternum to the ground (as when teaching the down), but then lure the dog to stand and offer the treat. On successive trials, gradually increase the length of time the dog is required to remain in the playbow posture in order to gain a food reward. If the dog's rear end collapses into a down, say nothing and offer no reward; simply start over.

BE A BEAR

With the dog sitting backed into a corner to prevent him from toppling over backwards, say "Be a Bear!" With bent paw and palm down, raise a lure upwards and backwards along the top of the dog's muzzle. Praise the dog when he sits up on his haunches and offer the treat as a reward. To prevent the dog from standing on his hind legs, keep the lure closer to the dog's muzzle. On each trial, progressively increase the length of time the dog is required to sit up to receive a food reward. Since lure/reward training is so easy, teach the dog to stand and walk on his hind legs as well!

Teaching "Be a Bear"

chapter 9

Getting
Active
with your Dog

by Bardi McLennan

Once you and your dog have graduated from basic obedience training and are beginning to work together as a team, you can take part in the growing world of dog activities. There are so many fun things to do with your dog! Just remember, people and dogs don't always learn at the same pace, so don't be upset if you (or your dog) need more than two basic training courses before your team becomes operational. Even smart dogs don't go straight to college from kindergarten!

Just as there are events geared to certain types of dogs, so there are ones that are more appealing to certain types of people. In some

128

activities, you give the commands and your dog does the work (upland game hunting is one example), while in others, such as agility, you'll both get a workout. You may want to aim for prestigious titles to add to your dog's name, or you may want nothing more than the sheer enjoyment of being around other people and their dogs. Passive or active, participation has its own rewards.

Consider your dog's physical capabilities when looking into any of the canine activities. It's easy to see that a Basset Hound is not built for the racetrack, nor would a Chihuahua be the breed of choice for pulling a sled. A loyal dog will attempt almost anything you ask him to do, so it is up to you to know your dog's limitations. A dog must be physically sound in order to compete at any level in athletic activities, and being mentally sound is a definite plus. Advanced age, however, may not be a deterrent. Many dogs still hunt and herd at ten or twelve years of age. It's entirely possible for dogs to be "fit at 50." Take your dog for a checkup, explain to your vet the type of activity you have in mind and be guided by his or her findings.

All dogs seem to love playing flyball.

You needn't be restricted to breed-specific sports if it's only fun you're after. Certain AKC activities are limited to designated breeds; however, as each new trial, test or sport has grown in popularity, so has the variety of breeds encouraged to participate at a fun level.

But don't shortchange your fun, or that of your dog, by thinking only of the basic function of her breed. Once a dog has learned how to learn, she can be taught to do just about anything as long as the size of the dog is right for the job and you both think it is fun and rewarding. In other words, you are a team.

To get involved in any of the activities detailed in this chapter, look for the names and addresses of the organizations that sponsor them in Chapter 13. You can also ask your breeder or a local dog trainer for contacts.

You can compete in obedience trials with a well trained dog.

Official American Kennel Club Activities

The following tests and trials are some of the events sanctioned by the AKC and sponsored by various dog clubs. Your dog's expertise will be rewarded with impressive titles. You can participate just for fun, or be competitive and go for those awards.

OBEDIENCE

Training classes begin with pups as young as three months of age in kindergarten puppy training, then advance to pre-novice (all exercises on lead) and go on to novice, which is where you'll start off-lead work. In obedience classes dogs learn to sit, stay, heel and come through a variety of exercises. Once you've got the basics down, you can enter obedience trials and work toward earning your dog's first degree, a C.D. (Companion Dog).

The next level is called "Open," in which jumps and retrieves perk up the dog's interest. Passing grades in competition at this level earn a C.D.X. (Companion Dog Excellent). Beyond that lies the goal of the most ambitious—Utility (U.D. and even U.D.X. or OTCh, an Obedience Champion).

AGILITY

All dogs can participate in the latest canine sport to have gained worldwide popularity for its fun and excitement, agility. It began in England as a canine version of horse show-jumping, but because dogs are more agile and able to perform on verbal commands, extra feats were added such as climbing, balancing and racing through tunnels or in and out of weave poles.

Many of the obstacles (regulation or homemade) can be set up in your own backyard. If the agility bug bites, you could end up in international competition!

For starters, your dog should be obedience trained, even though, in the beginning, the lessons may all be taught on lead. Once the dog understands the commands (and you do, too), it's as easy as guiding the dog over a prescribed course, one obstacle at a time. In competition, the race is against the clock, so wear your running shoes! The dog starts with 200 points and the judge deducts for infractions and misadventures along the way.

All dogs seem to love agility and respond to it as if they were being turned loose in a playground paradise. Your dog's enthusiasm will be contagious; agility turns into great fun for dog and owner.

FIELD TRIALS AND HUNTING TESTS

There are field trials and hunting tests for the sporting breeds—retrievers, spaniels and pointing breeds, and for some hounds—Bassets, Beagles and Dachshunds. Field trials are competitive events that test a dog's ability to perform the functions for which she was bred. Hunting tests, which are open to retrievers,

Getting Active with Your Dog

TITLES AWARDED BY THE AKC

Conformation: Ch. (Champion)

Obedience: CD (Companion Dog); CDX (Companion Dog Excellent); UD (Utility Dog); UDX (Utility Dog Excellent); OTCh. (Obedience Trial Champion)

Field: JH (Junior Hunter); SH (Senior Hunter); MH (Master Hunter); AFCh. (Amateur Field Champion); FCh. (Field Champion)

Lure Coursing: JC (Junior Courser); SC (Senior Courser)

Herding: HT (Herding Tested); PT (Pre-Trial Tested); HS (Herding Started); HI (Herding Intermediate); HX (Herding Excellent); HCh. (Herding Champion)

Tracking: TD (Tracking Dog); TDX (Tracking Dog Excellent)

Agility: NAD (Novice Agility); OAD (Open Agility); ADX (Agility Excellent); MAX (Master Agility)

Earthdog Tests: JE (Junior Earthdog); SE (Senior Earthdog); ME (Master Earthdog)

Canine Good Citizen: CGC

Combination: DC (Dual Champion—Ch. and Fch.); TC (Triple Champion—Ch., Fch., and OTCh.)

131

spaniels and pointing breeds only, are noncompetitive and are a means of judging the dog's ability as well as that of the handler.

Hunting is a very large and complex part of canine sports, and if you own one of the breeds that hunts, the events are a great treat for your dog and you. He gets to do what he was bred for, and you get to work with him and watch him do it. You'll be proud of and amazed at what your dog can do.

Retrievers and other sporting breeds get to do what they're bred to in hunting tests.

Fortunately, the AKC publishes a series of booklets on these events, which outline the rules and regulations and include a glossary of the sometimes complicated terms. The AKC also publishes newsletters for field trialers and hunting test enthusiasts. The United Kennel Club (UKC) also has informative materials for the hunter and his dog.

HERDING TESTS AND TRIALS

Herding, like hunting, dates back to the first known uses man made of dogs. The interest in herding today is widespread, and if you own a herding breed, you can join in the activity. Herding dogs are tested for their natural skills to keep a flock of ducks, sheep or cattle together. If your dog shows potential, you can start at the testing level, where your dog can earn a title for showing an inherent herding ability. With training you can advance to the trial level, where your dog should be capable of controlling even difficult livestock in diverse situations.

LURE COURSING

The AKC Tests and Trials for Lure Coursing are open to traditional sighthounds—Greyhounds, Whippets,

Borzoi, Salukis, Afghan Hounds, Ibizan Hounds and Scottish Deerhounds—as well as to Basenjis and Rhodesian Ridgebacks. Hounds are judged on overall ability, follow, speed, agility and endurance. This is possibly the most exciting of the trials for spectators, because the speed and agility of the dogs is awesome to watch as they chase the lure (or "course") in heats of two or three dogs at a time.

TRACKING

Tracking is another activity in which almost any dog can compete because every dog that sniffs the ground when taken outdoors is, in fact, tracking. The hard part comes when the rules as to what, when and where the dog tracks are determined by a person, not the dog! Tracking tests cover a large area of fields, woods and roads. The tracks are laid hours before the dogs go to work on them, and include "tricks" like cross-tracks and sharp turns. If you're interested in search-and-rescue work, this is the place to start.

This tracking dog is hot on the trail.

EARTHDOG TESTS FOR SMALL TERRIERS AND DACHSHUNDS

These tests are open to Australian, Bedlington, Border, Cairn, Dandie Dinmont, Smooth and Wire Fox, Lakeland, Norfolk, Norwich, Scottish, Sealyham, Skye, Welsh and West Highland White Terriers as well as Dachshunds. The dogs need no prior training for this terrier sport. There is a qualifying test on the day of the event, so dog and handler learn the rules on the spot. These tests, or "digs," sometimes end with informal races in the late afternoon.

Here are some of the extracurricular obedience and racing activities that are not regulated by the AKC or UKC, but are generally run by clubs or a group of dog fanciers and are often open to all.

Canine Freestyle This activity is something new on the scene and is variously likened to dancing, dressage or ice skating. It is meant to show the athleticism of the dog, but also requires showmanship on the part of the dog's handler. If you and your dog like to ham it up for friends, you might want to look into freestyle.

Lure coursing lets sighthounds do what they do best—run!

Scent Hurdle Racing Scent hurdle racing is purely a fun activity sponsored by obedience clubs with members forming competing teams. The height of the hurdles is based on the size of the shortest dog on the team. On a signal, one team dog is released on each of two side-by-side courses and must clear every hurdle before picking up its own dumbbell from a platform and returning over the jumps to the handler. As each dog returns, the next on that team is sent. Of course, that is what the dogs are supposed to do. When the dogs improvise (going under or around the hurdles, stealing another dog's dumbbell, and so forth), it no doubt frustrates the handlers, but just adds to the fun for everyone else.

Flyball This type of racing is similar, but after negotiating the four hurdles, the dog comes to a flyball box, steps on a lever that releases a tennis ball into the air, catches the ball and returns over the hurdles to the starting point. This game also becomes extremely fun for spectators because the dogs sometimes cheat by catching a ball released by the dog in the next lane. Three titles can be earned—Flyball Dog (F.D.), Flyball Dog Excellent (F.D.X.) and Flyball Dog Champion (Fb.D.Ch.)—all awarded by the North American Flyball Association, Inc.

Dogsledding The name conjures up the Rocky Mountains or the frigid North, but you can find dogsled clubs in such unlikely spots as Maryland, North Carolina and Virginia! Dogsledding is primarily for the Nordic breeds such as the Alaskan Malamutes, Siberian Huskies and Samoyeds, but other breeds can try. There are some practical backyard applications to this sport, too. With parental supervision, almost any strong dog could pull a child's sled.

Coming over the A-frame on an agility course.

These are just some of the many recreational ways you can get to know and understand your multifaceted dog better and have fun doing it.

chapter 10

Your Dog
and your
Family

by Bardi McLennan

Adding a dog automatically increases your family by one, no matter whether you live alone in an apartment or are part of a mother, father and six kids household. The single-person family is fair game for numerous and varied canine misconceptions as to who is dog and who pays the bills, whereas a dog in a houseful of children will consider himself to be just one of the gang, littermates all. One dog and one child may give a dog reason to believe they are both kids or both dogs. Either interpretation requires parental supervision and sometimes speedy intervention.

As soon as one paw goes through the door into your home, Rufus (or Rufina) has to make many adjustments to become a part of your family. Your job is to make him fit in as painlessly as possible. An older dog may have some frame of reference from past experience, but to a 10-week-old puppy, everything is brand new: people, furniture, stairs, when and where people eat, sleep or watch TV, his own place and everyone else's space, smells, sounds, outdoors—everything!

Puppies, and newly acquired dogs of any age, do not need what we think of as "freedom." If you leave a new dog or puppy loose in the house, you will almost certainly return to chaotic destruction and the dog will forever after equate your homecoming with a time of punishment to be dreaded. It is unfair to give your dog what amounts to "freedom to get into trouble." Instead, confine him to a crate for brief periods of your absence (up to three or four hours) and, for the long haul, a workday for example, confine him to one untrashable area with his own toys, a bowl of water and a radio left on (low) in another room.

Lots of pets get along with each other just fine.

For the first few days, when not confined, put Rufus on a long leash tied to your wrist or waist. This umbilical cord method enables the dog to learn all about you from your body language and voice, and to learn by his own actions which things in the house are NO! and which ones are rewarded by "Good dog." House-training will be easier with the pup always by your side. Speaking of which, accidents do happen. That goal of "completely housetrained" takes up to a year, or the length of time it takes the pup to mature.

The All-Adult Family

Most dogs in an adults-only household today are likely to be latchkey pets, with no one home all day but the dog. When you return after a tough day on the job, the dog can and should be your relaxation therapy. But going home can instead be a daily frustration.

Separation anxiety is a very common problem for the dog in a working household. It may begin with whines and barks of loneliness, but it will soon escalate into a frenzied destruction derby. That is why it is so important to set aside the time to teach a dog to relax when left alone in his confined area and to understand that he can trust you to return.

Let the dog get used to your work schedule in easy stages. Confine him to one room and go in and out of that room over and over again. Be casual about it. No physical, voice or eye contact. When the pup no longer even notices your comings and goings, leave the house for varying lengths of time, returning to stay home for a few minutes and gradually increasing the time away. This training can take days, but the dog is learning that you haven't left him forever and that he can trust you.

Any time you leave the dog, but especially during this training period, be casual about your departure. No anxiety-building fond farewells. Just "Bye" and go! Remember the "Good dog" when you return to find everything more or less as you left it.

If things are a mess (or even a disaster) when you return, greet the dog, take him outside to eliminate, and then put him in his crate while you clean up. Rant and rave in the shower! *Do not* punish the dog. You were not there when it happened, and the rule is: Only punish as you catch the dog in the act of wrongdoing. Obviously, it makes sense to get your latchkey puppy when you'll have a week or two to spend on these training essentials.

Family weekend activities should include Rufus whenever possible. Depending on the pup's age, now is the time for a long walk in the park, playtime in the backyard, a hike in the woods. Socializing is as important as health care, good food and physical exercise, so visiting Aunt Emma or Uncle Harry and the next-door neighbor's dog or cat is essential to developing an outgoing, friendly temperament in your pet.

If you are a single adult, socializing Rufus at home and away will prevent him from becoming overly protective of you (or just overly attached) and will also prevent such behavioral problems as dominance or fear of strangers.

Babies

Whether already here or on the way, babies figure larger than life in the eyes of a dog. If the dog is there first, let him in on all your baby preparations in the house. When baby arrives, let Rufus sniff any item of clothing that has been on the baby before Junior comes home. Then let Mom greet the dog first before introducing the new family member. Hold the baby down for the dog to see and sniff, but make sure someone's holding the dog on lead in case of any sudden moves. Don't play keep-away or tease the dog with the baby, which only invites undesirable jumping up.

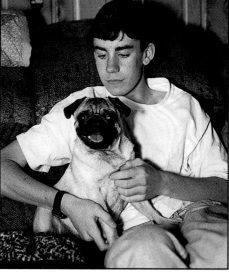

The dog and the baby are "family," and for starters can be treated almost as equals. Things rapidly change, however, especially when baby takes to creeping around on all fours on the dog's turf or, better yet, has yummy pudding all over her face and hands! That's when a lot of things in the dog's and baby's lives become more separate than equal.

Dogs are perfect confidants.

Toddlers make terrible dog owners, but if you can't avoid the combination, use patient discipline (that is, positive teaching rather than punishment), and use time-outs before you run out of patience.

A dog and a baby (or toddler, or an assertive young child) should never be left alone together. Take the dog with you or confine him. With a baby or youngsters in the house, you'll have plenty of use for that wonderful canine safety device called a crate!

Young Children

Any dog in a house with kids will behave pretty much as the kids do, good or bad. But even good dogs and good children can get into trouble when play becomes rowdy and active.

Teach children how to play nicely with a puppy.

Legs bobbing up and down, shrill voices screeching, a ball hurtling overhead, all add up to exuberant frustration for a dog who's just trying to be part of the gang. In a pack of puppies, any legs or toys being chased would be caught by a set of teeth, and all the pups involved would understand that is how the game is played. Kids do not understand this, nor do parents tolerate it. Bring Rufus indoors before you have reason to regret it. This is time-out, not a punishment.

You can explain the situation to the children and tell them they must play quieter games until the puppy learns not to grab them with his mouth. Unfortunately, you can't explain it that easily to the dog. With adult supervision, they will learn how to play together.

Young children love to tease. Sticking their faces or wiggling their hands or fingers in the dog's face is teasing. To another person it might be just annoying, but it is threatening to a dog. There's another difference: We can make the child stop by an explanation, but the only way a dog can stop it is with a warning growl and then with teeth. Teasing is the major cause of children being bitten by their pets. Treat it seriously.

Older Children

The best age for a child to get a first dog is between the ages of 8 and 12. That's when kids are able to accept some real responsibility for their pet. Even so, take the child's vow of "I will never *ever* forget to feed (brush, walk, etc.) the dog" for what it's worth: a child's good intention at that moment. Most kids today have extra lessons, soccer practice, Little League, ballet, and so forth piled on top of school schedules. There will be many times when Mom will have to come to the dog's rescue. "I walked the dog for you so you can set the table for me" is one way to get around a missed appointment without laying on blame or guilt.

Kids in this age group make excellent obedience trainers because they are into the teaching/learning process themselves and they lack the self-consciousness of adults. Attending a dog show is something the whole family can enjoy, and watching Junior Showmanship may catch the eye of the kids. Older children can begin to get involved in many of the recreational activities that were reviewed in the previous chapter. Some of the agility obstacles, for example, can be set up in the backyard as a family project (with an adult making sure all the equipment is safe and secure for the dog).

Older kids are also beginning to look to the future, and may envision themselves as veterinarians or trainers or show dog handlers or writers of the next Lassie best-seller. Dogs are perfect confidants for these dreams. They won't tell a soul.

Other Pets

Introduce all pets tactfully. In a dog/cat situation, hold the dog, not the cat. Let two dogs meet on neutral turf—a stroll in the park or a walk down the street—with both on loose leads to permit all the normal canine ways of saying hello, including routine sniffing, circling, more sniffing, and so on. Small creatures such as hamsters, chinchillas or mice must be kept safe from their natural predators (dogs and cats).

Festive Family Occasions

Parties are great for people, but not necessarily for puppies. Until all the guests have arrived, put the dog in his crate or in a room where he won't be disturbed. A socialized dog can join the fun later as long as he's not underfoot, annoying guests or into the hors d'oeuvres.

There are a few dangers to consider, too. Doors opening and closing can allow a puppy to slip out unnoticed in the confusion, and you'll be organizing a search party instead of playing host or hostess. Party food and buffet service are not for dogs. Let Rufus party in his crate with a nice big dog biscuit.

At Christmas time, not only are tree decorations dangerous and breakable (and perhaps family heirlooms), but extreme caution should be taken with the lights, cords and outlets for the tree lights and any other festive lighting. Occasionally a dog lifts a leg, ignoring the fact that the tree is indoors. To avoid this, use a canine repellent, made for gardens, on the tree. Or keep him out of the tree room unless supervised. And whatever you do, *don't* invite trouble by hanging his toys on the tree!

Car Travel

Before you plan a vacation by car or RV with Rufus, be sure he enjoys car travel. Nothing spoils a holiday quicker than a carsick dog! Work within the dog's comfort level. Get in the car with the dog in his crate or attached to a canine car safety belt and just sit there until he relaxes. That's all. Next time, get in the car, turn on the engine and go nowhere. Just sit. When that is okay, turn on the engine and go around the block. Now you can go for a ride and include a stop where you get out, leaving the dog for a minute or two.

On a warm day, always park in the shade and leave windows open several inches. And return quickly. It only takes 10 minutes for a car to become an overheated steel death trap.

Motel or Pet Motel?

Not all motels or hotels accept pets, but you have a much better choice today than even a few years ago. To find a dog-friendly lodging, look at *On the Road Again With Man's Best Friend*, a series of directories that detail bed and breakfasts, inns, family resorts and other hotels/motels. Some places require a refundable deposit to cover any damage incurred by the dog. More B&Bs accept pets now, but some restrict the size.

If taking Rufus with you is not feasible, check out boarding kennels in your area. Your veterinarian may offer this service, or recommend a kennel or two he or she is familiar with. Go see the facilities for yourself, ask about exercise, diet, housing, and so on. Or, if you'd rather have Rufus stay home, look into bonded petsitters, many of whom will also bring in the mail and water your plants.

chapter 11

Your Dog
and your
Community

by Bardi McLennan

Step outside your home with your dog and you are no longer just family, you are both part of your community. This is when the phrase "responsible pet ownership" takes on serious implications. For starters, it means you pick up after your dog—not just occasionally, but every time your dog eliminates away from home. That means you have joined the Plastic Baggy Brigade! You always have plastic sandwich bags in your pocket and several in the car. It means you teach your kids how to use them, too. If you think this is "yucky," just imagine what the person (a non-doggy person) who inadvertently steps in the mess thinks!

Your responsibility extends to your neighbors: To their ears (no annoying barking); to their property (their garbage, their lawn, their flower beds, their cat—especially their cat); to their kids (on bikes, at play); to their kids' toys and sports equipment.

There are numerous dog-related laws, ranging from simple dog licensing and leash laws to those holding you liable for any physical injury or property damage done by your dog. These laws are in place to protect everyone in the community, including you and your dog. There are town ordinances and state laws which are by no means the same in all towns or all states. Ignorance of the law won't get you off the hook. The time to find out what the laws are where you live is now.

Be sure your dog's license is current. This is not just a good local ordinance, it can make the difference between finding your lost dog or not.

Dressing your dog up makes him appealing to strangers.

Many states now require proof of rabies vaccination and that the dog has been spayed or neutered before issuing a license. At the same time, keep up the dog's annual immunizations.

Never let your dog run loose in the neighborhood. This will not only keep you on the right side of the leash law, it's the outdoor version of the rule about not giving your dog "freedom to get into trouble."

Good Canine Citizen

Sometimes it's hard for a dog's owner to assess whether or not the dog is sufficiently socialized to be accepted by the community at large. Does Rufus or Rufina display good, controlled behavior in public? The AKC's Canine Good Citizen program is available through many dog organizations. If your dog passes the test, the title "CGC" is earned.

The overall purpose is to turn your dog into a good neighbor and to teach you about your responsibility to your community as a dog owner. Here are the ten things your dog must do willingly:

1. Accept a stranger stopping to chat with you.
2. Sit and be petted by a stranger.
3. Allow a stranger to handle him or her as a groomer or veterinarian would.
4. Walk nicely on a loose lead.
5. Walk calmly through a crowd.
6. Sit and down on command, then stay in a sit or down position while you walk away.
7. Come when called.
8. Casually greet another dog.
9. React confidently to distractions.
10. Accept being left alone with someone other than you and not become overly agitated or nervous.

Schools and Dogs

Schools are getting involved with pet ownership on an educational level. It has been proven that children who are kind to animals are humane in their attitude toward other people as adults.

A dog is a child's best friend, and so children are often primary pet owners, if not the primary caregivers. Unfortunately, they are also the ones most often bitten by dogs. This occurs due to a lack of understanding that pets, no matter how sweet, cuddly and loving, are still animals. Schools, along with parents, dog clubs, dog fanciers and the AKC, are working to change all that with video programs for children not only in grade school, but in the nursery school and pre-kindergarten age group. Teaching youngsters how to be responsible dog owners is important community work. When your dog has a CGC, volunteer to take part in an educational classroom event put on by your dog club.

Boy Scout Merit Badge

A Merit Badge for Dog Care can be earned by any Boy
Scout ages 11 to 18. The requirements are not easy, but
amount to a complete course in responsible dog care
and general ownership. Here are just a few of the
things a Scout must do to earn that badge:

Point out ten parts of the dog using the correct
names.

Give a report (signed by parent or guardian) on
your care of the dog (feeding, food used, housing,
exercising, grooming and bathing), plus what has
been done to keep the dog healthy.

Explain the right way to obedience train a dog,
and demonstrate three comments.

Several of the requirements have to do with health
care, including first aid, handling a hurt dog, and
the dangers of home treatment for a serious
ailment.

The final requirement is to know the local laws
and ordinances involving dogs.

There are similar programs for Girl Scouts and 4-H
members.

Local Clubs

Local dog clubs are no longer in existence just to put
on a yearly dog show. Today, they are apt to be the hub
of the community's involvement with pets. Dog clubs
conduct educational forums with big-name speakers,
stage demonstrations of canine talent in a busy mall
and take dogs of various breeds to schools for classroom discussion.

The quickest way to feel accepted as a member in a
club is to volunteer your services! Offer to help with
something—anything—and watch your popularity
(and your interest) grow.

Therapy Dogs

Once your dog has earned that essential CGC and reliably demonstrates a steady, calm temperament, you could look into what therapy dogs are doing in your area.

Therapy dogs go with their owners to visit patients at hospitals or nursing homes, generally remaining on leash but able to coax a pat from a stiffened hand, a smile from a blank face, a few words from sealed lips or a hug from someone in need of love.

Your dog can make a difference in lots of lives.

Nursing homes cover a wide range of patient care. Some specialize in care of the elderly, some in the treatment of specific illnesses, some in physical therapy. Children's facilities also welcome visits from trained therapy dogs for boosting morale in their pediatric patients. Hospice care for the terminally ill and the at-home care of AIDS patients are other areas where this canine visiting is desperately needed. Therapy dog training comes first.

There is a lot more involved than just taking your nice friendly pooch to someone's bedside. Doing therapy dog work involves your own emotional stability as well as that of your dog. But once you have met all the requirements for this work, making the rounds once a week or once a month with your therapy dog is possibly the most rewarding of all community activities.

Disaster Aid

This community service is definitely not for everyone, partly because it is time-consuming. The initial training is rigorous, and there can be no let-up in the continuing workouts, because members are on call 24 hours a day to go wherever they are needed at a moment's notice. But if you think you would like to be able to assist in a disaster, look into search-and-rescue work. The network of search-and-rescue volunteers is worldwide, and all members of the American Rescue Dog Association (ARDA) who are qualified to do this work are volunteers who train and maintain their own dogs.

Physical Aid

Most people are familiar with Seeing Eye dogs, which serve as blind people's eyes, but not with all the other work that dogs are trained to do to assist the disabled. Dogs are also specially trained to pull wheelchairs, carry school books, pick up dropped objects, open and close doors. Some also are ears for the deaf. All these assistance-trained dogs, by the way, are allowed anywhere "No Pet" signs exist (as are therapy dogs when

Making the rounds with your therapy dog can be very rewarding.

properly identified). Getting started in any of this fascinating work requires a background in dog training and canine behavior, but there are also volunteer jobs ranging from answering the phone to cleaning out kennels to providing a foster home for a puppy. You have only to ask.

part four

Beyond the Basics

chapter 12

Recommended Reading

Books

ABOUT HEALTH CARE

Ackerman, Lowell. *Guide to Skin and Haircoat Problems in Dogs*. Loveland, Colo.: Alpine Publications, 1994.

Alderton, David. *The Dog Care Manual*. Hauppauge, N.Y.: Barron's Educational Series, Inc., 1986.

American Kennel Club. *American Kennel Club Dog Care and Training*. New York: Howell Book House, 1991.

Bamberger, Michelle, DVM. *Help! The Quick Guide to First Aid for Your Dog*. New York: Howell Book House, 1995.

Carlson, Delbert, DVM, and James Giffin, MD. *Dog Owner's Home Veterinary Handbook*. New York: Howell Book House, 1992.

DeBitetto, James, DVM, and Sarah Hodgson. *You & Your Puppy*. New York: Howell Book House, 1995.

Humphries, Jim, DVM. *Dr. Jim's Animal Clinic for Dogs*. New York: Howell Book House, 1994.

McGinnis, Terri. *The Well Dog Book*. New York: Random House, 1991.

Pitcairn, Richard and Susan. *Natural Health for Dogs*. Emmaus, Pa.: Rodale Press, 1982.

ABOUT DOG SHOWS

Hall, Lynn. *Dog Showing for Beginners*. New York: Howell Book House, 1994.

Nichols, Virginia Tuck. *How to Show Your Own Dog*. Neptune, N. J.: TFH, 1970.

Vanacore, Connie. *Dog Showing, An Owner's Guide*. New York: Howell Book House, 1990.

ABOUT TRAINING

Ammen, Amy. *Training in No Time.* New York: Howell Book House, 1995.

Baer, Ted. *Communicating With Your Dog.* Hauppauge, N.Y.: Barron's Educational Series, Inc., 1989.

Benjamin, Carol Lea. *Dog Problems.* New York: Howell Book House, 1989.

Benjamin, Carol Lea. *Dog Training for Kids.* New York: Howell Book House, 1988.

Benjamin, Carol Lea. *Mother Knows Best.* New York: Howell Book House, 1985.

Benjamin, Carol Lea. *Surviving Your Dog's Adolescence.* New York: Howell Book House, 1993.

Bohnenkamp, Gwen. *Manners for the Modern Dog.* San Francisco: Perfect Paws, 1990.

Dibra, Bashkim. *Dog Training by Bash.* New York: Dell, 1992.

Dunbar, Ian, PhD, MRCVS. *Dr. Dunbar's Good Little Dog Book,* James & Kenneth Publishers, 2140 Shattuck Ave. #2406, Berkeley, Calif. 94704. (510) 658–8588. Order from the publisher.

Dunbar, Ian, PhD, MRCVS. *How to Teach a New Dog Old Tricks,* James & Kenneth Publishers. Order from the publisher; address above.

Dunbar, Ian, PhD, MRCVS, and Gwen Bohnenkamp. Booklets on *Preventing Aggression; Housetraining; Chewing; Digging; Barking; Socialization; Fearfulness; and Fighting,* James & Kenneth Publishers. Order from the publisher; address above.

Evans, Job Michael. *People, Pooches and Problems.* New York: Howell Book House, 1991.

Kilcommons, Brian and Sarah Wilson. *Good Owners, Great Dogs.* New York: Warner Books, 1992.

McMains, Joel M. *Dog Logic—Companion Obedience.* New York: Howell Book House, 1992.

Rutherford, Clarice and David H. Neil, MRCVS. *How to Raise a Puppy You Can Live With.* Loveland, Colo.: Alpine Publications, 1982.

Volhard, Jack and Melissa Bartlett. *What All Good Dogs Should Know: The Sensible Way to Train.* New York: Howell Book House, 1991.

ABOUT BREEDING

Harris, Beth J. Finder. *Breeding a Litter, The Complete Book of Prenatal and Postnatal Care.* New York: Howell Book House, 1983.

Holst, Phyllis, DVM. *Canine Reproduction.* Loveland, Colo.: Alpine Publications, 1985.

Walkowicz, Chris and Bonnie Wilcox, DVM. *Successful Dog Breeding, The Complete Handbook of Canine Midwifery*. New York: Howell Book House, 1994.

ABOUT ACTIVITIES

American Rescue Dog Association. *Search and Rescue Dogs*. New York: Howell Book House, 1991.

Barwig, Susan and Stewart Hilliard. *Schutzhund*. New York: Howell Book House, 1991.

Beaman, Arthur S. *Lure Coursing*. New York: Howell Book House, 1994.

Daniels, Julie. *Enjoying Dog Agility—From Backyard to Competition*. New York: Doral Publishing, 1990.

Davis, Kathy Diamond. *Therapy Dogs*. New York: Howell Book House, 1992.

Gallup, Davis Anne. *Running With Man's Best Friend*. Loveland, Colo.: Alpine Publications, 1986.

Habgood, Dawn and Robert. *On the Road Again With Man's Best Friend*. New England, Mid-Atlantic, West Coast and Southeast editions. Selective guides to area bed and breakfasts, inns, hotels and resorts that welcome guests and their dogs. New York: Howell Book House, 1995.

Holland, Vergil S. *Herding Dogs*. New York: Howell Book House, 1994.

LaBelle, Charlene G. *Backpacking With Your Dog*. Loveland, Colo.: Alpine Publications, 1993.

Simmons-Moake, Jane. *Agility Training, The Fun Sport for All Dogs*. New York: Howell Book House, 1991.

Spencer, James B. *Hup! Training Flushing Spaniels the American Way*. New York: Howell Book House, 1992.

Spencer, James B. *Point! Training the All-Seasons Birddog*. New York: Howell Book House, 1995.

Tarrant, Bill. *Training the Hunting Retriever*. New York: Howell Book House, 1991.

Volhard, Jack and Wendy. *The Canine Good Citizen*. New York: Howell Book House, 1994.

General Titles

Haggerty, Captain Arthur J. *How to Get Your Pet Into Show Business*. New York: Howell Book House, 1994.

McLennan, Bardi. *Dogs and Kids, Parenting Tips*. New York: Howell Book House, 1993.

Moran, Patti J. *Pet Sitting for Profit, A Complete Manual for Professional Success*. New York: Howell Book House, 1992.

Scalisi, Danny and Libby Moses. *When Rover Just Won't Do, Over 2,000 Suggestions for Naming Your Dog.* New York: Howell Book House, 1993.

Sife, Wallace, PhD. *The Loss of a Pet.* New York: Howell Book House, 1993.

Wrede, Barbara J. *Civilizing Your Puppy.* Hauppauge, N.Y.: Barron's Educational Series, 1992.

Magazines

The AKC GAZETTE, The Official Journal for the Sport of Purebred Dogs. American Kennel Club, 51 Madison Ave., New York, NY.

Bloodlines Journal. United Kennel Club, 100 E. Kilgore Rd., Kalamazoo, MI.

Dog Fancy. Fancy Publications, 3 Burroughs, Irvine, CA 92718

Dog World. Maclean Hunter Publishing Corp., 29 N. Wacker Dr., Chicago, IL 60606.

Videos

"SIRIUS Puppy Training," by Ian Dunbar, PhD, MRCVS. James & Kenneth Publishers, 2140 Shattuck Ave. #2406, Berkeley, CA 94704. Order from the publisher.

"Training the Companion Dog," from Dr. Dunbar's British TV Series, James & Kenneth Publishers. (See address above).

The American Kennel Club produces videos on every breed of dog, as well as on hunting tests, field trials and other areas of interest to purebred dog owners. For more information, write to AKC/Video Fulfillment, 5580 Centerview Dr., Suite 200, Raleigh, NC 27606.

chapter 13

Resources

Breed Clubs

Every breed recognized by the American Kennel Club has a national (parent) club. National clubs are a great source of information on your breed. You can get the name of the secretary of the club by contacting:

The American Kennel Club
51 Madison Avenue
New York, NY 10010
(212) 696-8200

There are also numerous all-breed, individual breed, obedience, hunting and other special-interest dog clubs across the country. The American Kennel Club can provide you with a geographical list of clubs to find ones in your area. Contact them at the above address.

Registry Organizations

Registry organizations register purebred dogs. The American Kennel Club is the oldest and largest in this country, and currently recognizes over 130 breeds. The United Kennel Club registers some breeds the AKC doesn't (including the American Pit Bull Terrier and the Miniature Fox Terrier) as well as many of the same breeds. The others included here are for your reference; the AKC can provide you with a list of foreign registries.

American Kennel Club
51 Madison Avenue
New York, NY 10010

United Kennel Club (UKC)
100 E. Kilgore Road
Kalamazoo, MI 49001-5598

American Dog Breeders Assn.
P.O. Box 1771
Salt Lake City, UT 84110
(Registers American Pit Bull Terriers)

Canadian Kennel Club
89 Skyway Avenue
Etobicoke, Ontario
Canada M9W 6R4

National Stock Dog Registry
P.O. Box 402
Butler, IN 46721
(Registers working stock dogs)

Orthopedic Foundation for Animals (OFA)
2300 E. Nifong Blvd.
Columbia, MO 65201-3856
(Hip registry)

Activity Clubs

Write to these organizations for information on the
activities they sponsor.

American Kennel Club
51 Madison Avenue
New York, NY 10010
(Conformation Shows, Obedience Trials, Field
Trials and Hunting Tests, Agility, Canine Good

Citizen, Lure Coursing, Herding, Tracking,
Earthdog Tests, Coonhunting.)

United Kennel Club
100 E. Kilgore Road
Kalamazoo, MI 49001-5598
(Conformation Shows, Obedience Trials, Agility,
Hunting for Various Breeds, Terrier Trials and
more.)

North American Flyball Assn.
1342 Jeff St.
Ypsilanti, MI 48198

International Sled Dog Racing Assn.
P.O. Box 446
Norman, ID 83848-0446

North American Working Dog Assn., Inc.
Southeast Kreisgruppe
P.O. Box 833
Brunswick, GA 31521

Trainers

Association of Pet Dog Trainers
P.O. Box 3734
Salinas, CA 93912
(408) 663–9257

American Dog Trainers' Network
161 West 4th St.
New York, NY 10014
(212) 727–7257

**National Association of Dog Obedience
Instructors**
2286 East Steel Rd.
St. Johns, MI 48879

Associations

American Dog Owners Assn.
1654 Columbia Tpk.
Castleton, NY 12033
(Combats anti-dog legislation)

Delta Society
P.O. Box 1080
Renton, WA 98057-1080
(Promotes the human/animal bond through
pet-assisted therapy and other programs)

Dog Writers Assn. of America (DWAA)
Sally Cooper, Secy.
222 Woodchuck Ln.
Harwinton, CT 06791

National Assn. for Search and Rescue (NASAR)
P.O. Box 3709
Fairfax, VA 22038

Therapy Dogs International
6 Hilltop Road
Mendham, NJ 07945